Doorstep Democracy

Doorstep Democracy

FACE-TO-FACE POLITICS IN THE HEARTLAND

James H. Read

University of Minnesota Press
Minneapolis
London

Published by the University of Minnesota Press
111 Third Avenue South, Suite 290
Minneapolis, MN 55401-2520
http://www.upress.umn.edu

Library of Congress Cataloging-in-Publication Data

Read, James H., 1958–
    Doorstep democracy : face-to-face politics in the heartland / James H. Read.
        p.   cm.
    Includes bibliographical references.
    ISBN 978-0-8166-5679-0 (hc : alk. paper) — ISBN 978-0-8166-5680-6 (pb : alk. paper)
        1. Political campaigns—United States.   2. Political participation—United States.
    I. Title.
    JK2281.R43 2008
    324.70973—dc22

                                                            2008020781

Printed in the United States of America on acid-free paper

The University of Minnesota is an equal-opportunity educator and employer.

15 14 13 12 11 10 09 08   10 9 8 7 6 5 4 3 2 1

To Jim Graeve, Becky Hooper, and the memory of Bob Spaeth

The perverse and unorthodox argument of this little book is that voters are not fools.

— V. O. Key Jr., *The Responsible Electorate*

Contents

Political Campaigns as Conversation

We thrill once again to the all-absorbing leap-year spectacle of the presidential campaign. We ask ourselves, which candidate is the most charismatic orator? Which candidate was captured on camera making a face or refusing to shake hands? Or we fancy ourselves elite strategists ensconced in campaign war rooms, crunching poll numbers and manipulating delegate blocs like chess pieces.

Thus we imagine ourselves protagonists in the national democratic drama when in truth most of us are mere spectators. If democracy were only this glittering pageant, we would not have democracy at all; we would merely have elected kings and queens.

But there is another kind of democracy that takes place not in war rooms but outside front doors and around kitchen tables, a democracy not of focus-group-tested attack ads but of genuine face-to-face conversation between candidate and voter, a form of democracy so ancient and ordinary we risk overlooking it altogether. This ordinary but essential democracy is the focus of this book.

Every election year thousands of American citizens campaign for office by personally going door-to-door, engaging voters in face-to-face conversation and winning or losing the election one vote at a time. Because they do so, millions of American citizens regularly have the opportunity—which they may accept or decline—to ask candidates questions, directly judge their character, and hold them personally accountable. A doorstep exchange, even a brief one, gives candidate and voter an opportunity to persuade one another and learn from one another. That is what door-to-door campaigns for state legislative and local office provide, and this is the ordinary, but special, story I seek to tell in this book. The story deserves to be heard now more than ever because both campaign practice and the ordinary citizen's connection to politics are trending in so different a direction.

Conversation is probably not the best word to describe modern-day national campaigns. A contemporary presidential campaign, for instance, is more like a loudspeaker blaring through the windows of a house at full blast twenty-four hours a day. The occupants of the house can shut the windows and try to ignore the noise, but they cannot carry on a genuine conversation with the voice behind the loudspeaker. A candidate campaigning door-to-door for a low-profile legislative or local office (no TV, no mass media attention) in a presidential election year cannot compete with the loudspeakers. But he or she can (so to speak) walk quietly through the house, tap its occupants on the shoulder, momentarily turn their attention away from the loudspeakers, and begin a conversation—a reciprocal exchange, not a monologue.

I was a candidate in 1992 for the Minnesota House of Representatives in District 14A, a rural and small-town, socially conservative community near St. Cloud in central Minnesota. I lost the election by 98 votes out of 15,054 votes cast. The election was close enough to require a recount. When I lost the election, I returned to the projects and pursuits I had set aside to run for office.

My not-quite-successful campaign for office in small-town Minnesota some years ago is of little significance by itself. It matters only because it gave me the chance to experience, document, and reflect upon the kind of face-to-face politics essential to a healthy democracy. Many Americans who have run for state or local office could tell my story, or something like it, to their family and friends. But for some reason this ordinary activity has never been fully and properly explained—in writing and in detail—to the broader American public. There exist many how-to campaign manuals, of course. But these ignore the broader questions of why this kind of campaigning is worth doing in the first place, win or lose; how voters themselves learn and change from direct conversation with candidates; and how doorstep campaigning contributes to the health of democracy at every level, including our national campaigns.

So I dug into my personal archives. I resurrected hundreds of brief political conversations from handwritten notes scratched on a clipboard fifteen years ago. I reread old letters and questionnaires and listened to scratchy cassette tapes that miraculously still played. It was as though I was unearthing some fine old mansion buried beneath two decades of dust to discover that though the style had gone out of fashion, the foundations were as strong as ever.

The kind of campaign that monopolizes our attention, especially in presidential election years, is entirely different from the one described in this book. In contemporary presidential, statewide, and congressional campaigns most voters never meet the candidate, and mass-mediated communications flow only one way. State-of-the-art campaign strategy (increasingly even for legislative and local races) presupposes that voters can be classified, micro-targeted, emotionally manipulated, strategically turned out or strategically turned off, but not really persuaded to change their minds about anything of importance. And the rest of us adopt this political worldview whenever we speak of "red states" and "blue states" as though they were natural, unalterable facts.

I was a "blue" candidate in a "red" legislative district. I was a recent transplant to a close-knit community. My only competitive strategy was to meet people in person at their doorsteps, one or two individuals at a time, hear them out on the issues they cared about, and persuade them to vote for me. If I had won the race, I would have proceeded to the business of legislating, and this first campaign would have faded to the background; reelection campaigns would have become routine affairs rather than voyages of discovery. I never got the chance to participate in legislative deliberations. It is the deliberations with voters at the door that have endured in my memory and in my archives. And in a healthy democracy these deliberations are at least as important as what happens in the legislature.

I got into running for office almost by accident: not because I had any grand political ambitions, but because I didn't know how to say "No." I became chair of the local Democratic Farmer-Labor Party (the official name of the Democratic Party in Minnesota) because no one else was willing to do it. My principal responsibility as chair was to recruit candidates for office. I failed to persuade anyone else to run against a Republican incumbent in a district where the previous Democratic challenger had received only 32 percent of the vote. So I volunteered myself as the candidate. In an age where local political and civic participation has suffered a long decline (as documented in Robert Putnam's *Bowling Alone*), anyone who is willing to participate, even modestly, may find their level of engagement accelerating rapidly in this relative vacuum. Such was my own experience.

I teach in a political science department at a liberal arts college and, when I can find time, write books and articles on the history of American political thought. When I was studying political science at college and graduate school, I was sometimes asked whether this meant I intended to go into politics. I would smile and patiently explain that I was interested in political philosophy, which I considered much higher and purer than the low-level business of practical politics. When I thought about actual politics at all, it was "high-level" national and international politics, not state or local politics.

As a political theorist I had expended generous quantities of time and ink discoursing on the nature of democracy. But democracy as I studied it seemed pretty far removed from what I was doing in 1992: going door-to-door, fifty houses a day, six or seven days a week for six months, introducing myself to complete strangers, asking for their vote, trying somehow to engage them in conversation, then listening to their views (informed or uninformed) on a bafflingly wide range of issues including snowmobile license fees, workers' compensation, school funding, stoplights, nursing homes, medical costs, milk prices, taxes, Indian fishing rights, highway funds, groundwater contamination, Bill Clinton's sex life, and abortion, abortion, abortion. My political science education had not prepared me for this. I was a political theorist, not a public policy specialist; but even a policy wonk would be unprepared for the enormous range of matters on which a candidate for elective office is expected to have a position. I had to learn the issues on my feet: from conversations with voters at the door, from my own campaign volunteers, sometimes from the people working against me.

My training as a political theorist prepared me in only one crucial respect: I knew that all democracy rested on a foundation of citizen participation and political conversation and would die if that foundation crumbled. I routinely encouraged my students to participate in politics, and I would have been a hypocrite if I had failed to participate myself. I just did not know how quickly I would become addicted.

In the course of the campaign I engaged in substantive political *conversation* at approximately a third of the 7,500 households I visited. I wrote down what was said in these conversations, generating an archive of notes ten inches thick, which I preserved over the years and which constitutes the heart of this memoir. I kept and consulted many other documents to aid and correct my memory in writing this narrative: news articles, audiotapes, questionnaires from politically interested groups, campaign finance reports, my campaign literature and that of my opponent, letters I sent and letters sent to me.

When the U.S. Constitution was drafted in 1787, it included a clause specifying that the number of U.S. House of Representatives seats allocated to each state after the first national census "shall not exceed one for every thirty thousand" persons. Today there are approximately seven hundred thousand people in every congressional district, far more for the typical U.S. Senate or gubernatorial seat, and three hundred million people per U.S. president. It is almost impossible for any member of or candidate for Congress to get to know any more than a fraction—and probably the most ideologically committed or well-financed fraction—of the constituents he or she hopes to represent. The "public," to a member of the U.S. House, is in practice the public he or she actually knows, and this is a far from representative sample. For senators, governors, and presidents, the fraction is even smaller and more skewed by money and ideology.

But state legislative office, at least in most states, presents a very different picture. When I ran for the Minnesota Legislature, there were approximately thirty-three thousand people (including children) living in each house district—about the number of persons per *congressional* seat when the Constitution was ratified. Approximately twenty-two thousand of these people were of voting age. There were about ten thousand households. It is possible to speak personally with the majority of eligible voters in a district like this in a single election campaign if one works hard enough, and I did. In the course of such a campaign one encounters a wider and more representative sample of the people of the United States than one does campaigning for any higher office—and far wider than most people experience in their ordinary professional and family life, where the range of human beings we meet is pretty restricted. In campaigning for public office door-to-door I was forced to confront the entire range of human characters, with all their virtues and flaws, passions and interests, good ideas and bad ones.

Door-to-door campaigning is effective strategy where numbers and geography make it possible for a candidate to converse with a significant percentage of voters in the district. In most states this kind of campaigning could be practiced effectively in state legislative contests; Minnesota's constituent-representative ratio is fairly typical. According to 1999 data compiled by the National Conference of State Legislatures, twenty-five states had legislative house districts with fewer constituents per representative than Minnesota, and twenty-four had more. A few states had districts so small it would be no challenge at all for a candidate to meet nearly every voter, like New Hampshire (2,906 constituents per house district). In twenty-one states house district size fell between twenty thousand on one end and forty-five thousand on the other, making them broadly comparable to Minnesota (Alabama, Arkansas, Connecticut, Georgia, Hawaii, Idaho, Iowa, Kansas, Kentucky, Louisiana, Maryland, Massachusetts, Minnesota, Mississippi, Missouri, Nevada, New Mexico, Oklahoma, South Carolina, South Dakota, and Utah). In all these states candidates could personally contact the majority of households in the district if they chose a door-knocking campaign strategy. It equally follows that in all these states voters can, if they choose, *insist* that candidates campaign this way, rewarding those who do and punishing those who do not.

In about eight states (California, Florida, Illinois, New Jersey, New York, Ohio, Texas, and Washington) state house districts are so large—in some cases unnecessarily large—that it would be extremely difficult or impossible for legislative candidates to visit the majority of households. But door knocking can also be practiced in campaigns for local offices. What counts is the conversation itself; which level of campaign generates it is less important.

Some people get involved in politics only to be disillusioned by the experience. Others start out as cynics and have their cynicism reinforced. My own very intense contact with the electorate led me to agree with political scientist V. O. Key that "voters are not fools." In *The Responsible Electorate,* Key compares the voice of the people to an echo chamber. If voters act like children or fools, it is because candidates speak to them in childish or foolish ways. If candidates instead treat voters as rational and responsible adults, this is by and large how voters will behave.

In campaigning for office door-to-door, I myself looked for reasonable human beings and (with some exceptions) found them. I will not deny that I met many people who were very ignorant about or disconnected from politics. But as a candidate seeking their vote and inviting their conversation, I had an interest in treating political ignorance as a correctible problem.

This book is specifically written for two categories of readers: (1) people who have run for office, or worked on a campaign, or intend someday to do so; and (2) people who have never run for office, nor worked on a campaign, and never intend to do so. The narrative's relevance to people in the first category is obvious. The story is equally though less obviously directed to people in the second category.

Perhaps the most important lesson that prospective candidates can draw from my story is simply this: what a door-to-door campaign feels like from the candidate's perspective, and *why it is worth doing*—win or lose. This book is not a nuts-and-bolts campaign manual; prospective candidates can find that elsewhere.[1] I made my share of mistakes, and in any case campaign techniques and regulations have changed since 1992. But one particular campaign strategy is central to this narrative: door-to-door campaigning by the candidate in person. In a door-knocking–centered campaign, all other campaign activities—fund-raising, mailings, campaign Web sites, blogs, radio ads, endorsements, and so on—are important insofar as they make door knocking possible or reinforce its effects. Door knocking is an expensive campaign strategy—not in dollars but in scarce candidate time. Because money is often less scarce than time, many legislative candidates are tempted to resort to some more dollar-demanding (and indirect) but less time-consuming way of reaching voters. But for a candidate who wants to win and is able to budget the time, door knocking is good campaign strategy, at least where numbers and geography make it possible for the candidate to meet in person a critical mass of voters.

Of course, in many campaigns numbers make it impossible; this would include presidential, congressional, and gubernatorial campaigns and races in enormous state legislative districts like California's. But a large team of well-trained volunteers in a statewide race can engage the majority of voters in genuine conversation—if the campaign makes this a priority and considers it a winning strategy. A doorstep conversation between a voter and a campaign volunteer is not quite the same as a conversation between voter and candidate. Candidates in person at the door take direct responsibility for their own positions and are at liberty to revise their views in response to voters' arguments in a way volunteers representing the candidate are not. But if the goal is to treat voters as conversational partners rather than mere "targets," that ideal can be approximated to various degrees in any campaign.

When candidates engage in door knocking, they do not do it principally to elevate the level of civic engagement in the United States, but because they want to win the election. They judge that a personal conversation is more likely to sway an undecided voter than a mailing, e-mail, radio ad, scripted phone call, or literature drop. Yet in the process of campaigning this way—and especially if they spur their opponents to follow their lead—candidates reinvigorate the practice of democratic deliberation and forge the kind of bonds between voters and candidates a healthy democracy needs. Certainly there are other ways of campaigning, and indeed of winning, whose effects are less healthy.

The significance of this book for readers in the second category—those who have no intention of running for office or working on campaigns—is simply this: they represent the other side of the voter-candidate conversation, and it cannot occur without their consent. A candidate at the door cannot force genuine deliberation. He or she can only extend an invitation, which may be accepted or refused. During my own campaign I was impressed by the number of voters who welcomed conversation or at least tolerated it. Of course, in some cases habitual cynicism about politicians was a barrier to conversation. There is a certain irony in a voter's refusing to speak to a candidate at the door on the grounds that "politicians don't listen." If voters not only tolerated but demanded that candidates engage them in conversation—if they made this a condition of their vote—candidates for office would do more door knocking than they do now and practice it more conscientiously. Whether or not door knocking is a winning campaign strategy depends on the degree to which voters expect and reward it. If voters demand it, candidates will deliver it: that is my message to ordinary voters.

There has been much discussion lately of the low level of political discourse and civic engagement in the contemporary United States.[2] Fateful decisions are made with little or no public deliberation, attack ads are focus-group tested for maximum emotional effect, and twenty-four-hour-a-day satellite news conveys little of substance about either candidates or issues. Many of these pathologies in our democratic discourse have become institutionalized and difficult to change. But it would help at least to remind ourselves what an actual political conversation among reasonable people looks like. I believe that direct personal communications between candidates and voters, where numbers and scale make them possible, are worth attention as one possible restorative force in our democracy.

Other remedies have been proposed, some of which I examine in the book's conclusion, and I do not claim that door knocking alone will cure the disease. Some political theorists advocate a reinvigoration of town-meeting–style direct democracy, but only where small numbers make genuine deliberation possible, a scale much smaller than a Minnesota legislative district. Others advocate increased use of "citizen juries" and citizen task forces where a small group of ordinary citizens deliberates in depth on some policy problem and publicly announces its findings. Still others look to creative use of the Internet to stimulate citizen-citizen communications of a kind stifled by mass media politics. Almost all of these other strategies for enhancing democratic deliberation have received more attention, both in popular and academic circles, than old-fashioned door knocking.

All of these strategies have their advantages and drawbacks, and I do not claim that door knocking is the only way to increase the quantity and quality of citizen deliberation. Citizen task forces, for example, enable ordinary citizens to deliberate in much greater depth than is possible in a one-minute doorstep conversation, but door knocking draws into conversation a far larger number of citizens. And candidates for office have a far greater electoral interest in initiating doorstep conversations than in consulting the findings of citizen task forces.

The Internet was in its infancy as a tool of political communication when I ran for office in 1992. It has now become an essential venue for political fund-raising and for coordinating campaign activities. The advent of the blogosphere has made possible the rapid and unfiltered exchange of political information (or misinformation) and views among individuals who may never meet face-to-face. When people tell me they are skeptical that a political campaign from 1992 has any relevance today, they usually mention the Internet first.

But whatever else the Internet has changed, it has not significantly altered either the *practice* or the *value* of door knocking as a campaign technique. Creative use of the Internet by a state legislative campaign can supplement and reinforce personal contact but cannot adequately replace it. The Internet is a powerful tool for connecting like-minded people, as demonstrated by Howard Dean's innovative Internet fund-raising in the 2004 campaign. But the Internet tends to reinforce people's tendency to communicate principally to those with whom they already agree. In contrast, when one is door knocking, whether as candidate or campaign volunteer, one must regularly engage with people whose views differ from one's own. The undecided voters a local candidate most needs to reach and persuade are unlikely to initiate or respond to an electronic communication; in most cases they have to be first persuaded in person.

A good initial contact at doorstep or driveway can then be reinforced with subsequent e-mails and Web links. Internet-facilitated "meet-ups" can make it easier for politically energized citizens to gather in person to discuss issues and candidates. Internet meet-ups and campaign blogs also make it much easier for door-knocking–focused campaigns to coordinate place, time, and strategy. In all these ways the newest technology can reinforce old-fashioned face-to-face politics. But it is still the personal conversation that matters most. In this respect nothing has changed since 1992, and the story I tell is as current as ever. If we are genuinely interested in political deliberation by ordinary citizens, we should take a close look at the practice of door knocking: study it, encourage it, and improve it.

Genuine conversation between candidate and voter cannot be limited to easy issues. A door-knocking candidate invites dialogue on whatever the voter cares about and accepts the consequences of the invitation. I sometimes sighed with relief when a voter wanted to talk about schools or stoplights or affordable health insurance. But I was repeatedly drawn into difficult exchanges on abortion — precisely the issue on which many people insist no dialogue is possible. The title of chapter 5 suggests the mixed results of my willingness to engage in substantive debate on this issue. I could have simply said, "The Supreme Court has decided this" and declined to discuss the substance. But for better or worse, that is not the route I took. And given the real possibility that today's Supreme Court may reverse *Roe v. Wade* and give state legislatures increasing discretion to determine abortion policy, we may all find ourselves engaging in difficult deliberations about abortion, now with real policy consequences at stake. In this respect what I said and did and experienced in 1992 is perhaps even more significant now than it was then.

Every election year thousands of individuals run for state legislative office in the United States. Thousands more run for local office: city council, county board, school board, and so on. Campaigns that feature direct, reciprocal conversations between candidates and voters would seem to be an ordinary thing and for that very reason get overlooked. Such campaigns generate much personal oral history for those who participate in them, but are the subject of very few books. Bookstores are stocked instead with political memoirs (or exposés) of Washington insiders and high-level international heroes and villains.

But that something is ordinary does not make it unimportant or uninteresting. A piece of fruit illuminated by sunlight from a parlor window is an ordinary thing, but in the hands of a skilled painter it becomes something marvelous. My aim here is to paint the ordinary life of our democracy as it appeared to me through the small clear window of the voter's front door.

CHAPTER ONE

How I Got into This

It all began with the caucuses. I simply wanted to "get involved." I had no idea how involved I would get.

Minnesota's precinct caucuses intrigued me. I had never lived in a state that offered ordinary citizens any comparably intense form of political participation. I intended to be no more than a low-level participant, just enough to satisfy a political theorist's curiosity.

On the evening of Tuesday, February 27, 1990, I attended the Democratic Farmer-Labor Party caucus at Kennedy Elementary School in St. Joseph. (The Democratic Party in Minnesota is officially named the Democratic Farmer-Labor Party, or DFL; it was founded in 1944 with the merger of the Democratic and the Farmer-Labor parties.) I sat in a tiny chair intended for first-graders, discussed prospective Democratic U.S. Senate candidates, debated and voted on several resolutions, and ended up as a delegate to the County Unit Convention to be held on April 1 at Cold Spring Middle School.[1]

The local party conventions select delegates to the congressional district and state conventions, debate and vote on resolutions to be sent to the state convention, and serve as a ready-made audience of activists for candidates: U.S. Senate, governor, state party chair, U.S. Congress, and so on. But the first order of business was to elect a chair of the local party. There were no announced candidates. Six or seven nominations were made from the floor, all of which were refused by the nominees. The situation was becoming embarrassing: we had a gymnasium full of delegates with much important business to do, and none of it could proceed until someone agreed to be party chair.

Then Jane Bennett, whom I had met for the first time a few nights earlier at a League of Women Voters dinner, walked to the microphone and nominated me. She had not consulted me, and I was caught completely by surprise. I was flattered and accepted the nomination, hoping that more credible candidates would follow my lead. None did, and I was elected unanimously. For all anyone knew, I could have been a space alien—or worse, a Republican. What the more experienced delegates must have known, but I did not discover until later, was that the local party was divided and broken, and the new chair would face enormous obstacles. These obstacles were the combined result of the peculiar political character of rural Stearns County and of local and statewide party battles of the 1980s.

Stearns County is located in central Minnesota, with its eastern boundary on the Mississippi River about sixty miles northwest of Minneapolis.[2] Its small towns and farming communities were settled principally by Bavarian Catholic immigrants in the mid-nineteenth century, who also founded the monastic communities that sponsor the College of St. Benedict and St. John's University. Sauk Centre, the hometown of Sinclair Lewis and his model for *Main Street,* is in western Stearns County just outside the boundary of my legislative district. Garrison Keillor was living and working in rural Stearns County in the 1970s, and his fictional Lake Wobegon was inspired in large part by people, landscapes, churches, and cafés in my legislative district. (Lake Wobegon's German Catholics were drawn from life; Keillor's Norwegian Lutherans were fictionally supplied for good measure.)[3] Stearns County is one of the most productive dairy farming regions in the United States, and dairy farming remains its largest source of revenue, though only 11 percent of households earned income directly from farming in 1992.

Its German-Catholic-Bavarian heritage has made Stearns County more self-enclosed even than the typical small town and farming community. (The county's largest city, St. Cloud, is relatively more cosmopolitan by local standards, but it lay outside my legislative district.) In many Stearns County towns there is only one church, the Catholic Church, which is the center of its communal life. An exception is Holdingford, where there are two Catholic churches, originally one for the Germans and one for the Poles. In a state that has produced many noted internationalists, Stearns County was deeply isolationist through much of the twentieth century; in a state that took the lead on Prohibition, Stearns County was a bootlegging center. Politically it continues to go its own way. The part of Morrison County that lay within my legislative district (the county's southern tier of towns and townships) is very similar to Stearns County in its ethnic, economic, and religious profile.

In much of the United States, Catholic schools were formed as an alternative to the Protestant domination of the public schools. In Stearns County, on the other hand, the public schools were in effect Catholic parochial schools through most of the century. In 1990 the public elementary school in Avon (where I now live) was still in a building leased from the Catholic church next door, and Catholic religious imagery graced the classrooms and hallways of the school.[4]

Some of the locals, on discovering that I taught at the College of St. Benedict, were surprised to discover I was not a priest or monk; this was their image of Catholic universities. For me, as a non-Catholic, only quarter-German, religiously skeptical recent transplant to the county, all this was quite fascinating and new. It was odd, however, for me to discover that I had suddenly become a "local political leader" of such a community. That I could hope to represent this community in the legislature seemed beyond belief when I took over my duties as party chair in April 1990.

Political Stereotypes

Stearns County was perceived both by insiders and outsiders as a political, cultural, and religious monolith where almost everyone believed the same way on important matters, where parish priests called the political shots, and where you were considered a mere "transient" unless your grandparents were born there. Candidates for public office found it in their interest to campaign in ways that reinforced this stereotype, which like most stereotypes was partly true.

But there were a number of features about the district that challenged the monolithic stereotype. The number of residents who, like me, had moved into the district recently and who did not fit the traditional stereotype was significant and growing. Sartell, the largest city in the district (2,734 pre-election registered voters in 1992), was more like a newly sprung suburb of Minneapolis in its political and social profile; a large percentage of its residents were even newer to the district than I was. Just north of St. Joseph in St. Wendel Township lay Pleasant Acres, a new, unincorporated housing development whose population, many of them newcomers to Stearns County, exceeded that of most of the cities in the district. Yet almost the first thing many newcomers acquired, right after title to their property, was the prevalent idea that they had moved into a politically hidebound community where they were doomed to be marginal. So, ironically, the newcomers helped reinforce the very stereotype that shut them out.

The College of St. Benedict, where I teach, lay within my district (16A in 1990, 14A in 1992 after redistricting); St. John's University, where I also teach, lay in the B side of the same senate district.[5] Local political campaigns made little attempt to mobilize college students, and most faculty members viewed the Stearns County political scene with contempt if they thought about it at all. If faculty members and students could be persuaded to take local politics seriously, the university community could realize its hitherto slumbering potential to shape the political character of the district in ways that challenged the traditional stereotype.[6]

And as I was to discover in the course of my campaign, among Stearns County "old-timers" who fit the traditional demographic profile, there was more independence of mind than most insiders and outsiders gave them credit for. If rural and small-town Stearns County appeared a political monolith, it was partly because no one offered its voters any real choices in legislative contests; the stereotype was never put to the test.

Political parties were weak in the district. Many local voters were extravagantly suspicious of parties, and as a result most local candidates of both parties avoided visible use of party labels in their campaign literature and signs.

Of the three state legislative seats in the district for which I became responsible when I was elected chair in 1990, the one in which I lived, the 16A side of the senate district, was held by a Republican, Bernie Omann, while the other two were held by nominal Democrats: Joe Bertram held the senate seat, while his brother Jeff held the 16B house seat. But both Bertram brothers would have been more accurately designated conservative independents. They had little use for the local Democratic Party, which they did nothing to build and sustain. In their campaigning they conspicuously distanced themselves from the state and national Democratic tickets, and as a result were able to win by large majorities in districts where statewide Democratic candidates lost by large majorities. In 1990, for instance, Joe Bertram won his state senate race with 78 percent of the vote; Democratic U.S. Senate candidate Paul Wellstone received only 41 percent in the same district, though he won statewide. So far as the Bertram brothers positioned themselves on issues at all, it was to proclaim themselves 100 percent pro-life and 100 percent anti–gun control. Their real source of power lay in constituent service: helping people adopt babies, pressing agencies to grant their supporters and contributors exemptions from rules and regulations, showing up at every wedding and funeral, and sending personalized letters on the occasion of every birth and graduation in the district. As a result they were able to build up an impressively powerful and well-funded local political machine that had little connection with the local Democratic Party.[7]

I later discovered there was a darker side to the workings of the Bertram machine, but I did not know this at the time, and as newly elected party chair in 1990 and again as candidate for office in 1992 I did my best to work with them. They in turn supported (at least publicly) my party-building efforts as chair, though they must have also perceived a potential threat in what I was doing.

Abortion Politics

Far stronger and better organized than any political party in the district was the Minnesota Citizens Concerned for Life (MCCL), the most politically powerful pro-life organization in the state. The MCCL's ultimate political goal, as set forth in resolutions regularly introduced by its supporters at Democratic and Republican precinct caucuses, is to achieve a "Human Life Amendment to protect life from conception to natural death," that is, to outlaw all abortions. At any given time the MCCL has a number of more immediate abortion-related initiatives on its agenda, but it makes its ultimate goal clear.

What especially distinguishes the MCCL from other pro-life groups are its political tactics. Its impressive network of supporters publicly identify themselves with signs and posters, vote on that issue alone, turn out at high rates on election day, and urge their issue at every public forum and whenever a candidate shows up at their door. They can be mobilized on short notice to put intense pressure on officeholders and candidates, and at least in my district were far more effective than any political party in getting their endorsed candidates elected and their perceived enemies defeated. The MCCL is active everywhere in the state; what distinguished our district was that when I took over as Democratic Party chair, the MCCL was the *only* visible and effective political organization, without competitors. The local Republican Party was, with only slight exaggeration, a subcommittee of the MCCL.[8] The local Democratic Party was disorganized and paralyzed by divisions over abortion. The lack of organized political competition in our district helped reinforce the MCCL's own claim that its values and goals *were* the values and goals of the community, without dissent.

This picture of the entire community, minus a few renegades, united by uncompromising opposition to abortion was in fact a false one. Surveys conducted by Steve Frank of the political science department at St. Cloud State University indicated that views on the issue in Stearns County were measurably, but not dramatically, more antiabortion than the state as a whole.[9] In Stearns County, as in Minnesota and the United States generally, most residents' views on abortion fell somewhere in between the polar positions represented by activists and written into the Republican and Democratic platforms. Even in Stearns County the percentage of residents who agreed with the MCCL's absolute prohibitionist position was nowhere close to a majority. Yet in politics a passionately committed and effectively organized minority is typically more powerful than an unorganized and ideologically diverse majority, and on the abortion issue in rural Stearns County this had certainly been the case.

The MCCL's goal in election years, at least in districts like ours, was to ensure that *all* candidates for public office, whatever their party affiliation, declared themselves to be "100 percent pro-life," which at the same time indicated a willingness to follow the MCCL's political lead. (The advice handed down to new candidates by those previously elected in the district was to give the MCCL everything it asked for on its questionnaire, and to attend its annual banquet.) If all candidates for office declare themselves "100 percent pro-life," then the MCCL wins either way and reinforces the image of an unquestionable pro-life consensus in the community. And in this respect the organization had indeed been effective in rural Stearns and Morrison counties. Before I ran for office in 1992, no one, so far as I know, had ever run for state legislative office (much less won) in rural Stearns County who did not publicly endorse the MCCL's absolute prohibitionist position.

For the MCCL, it is not enough that a legislator vote its way on abortion legislation. Anyone who wants its continued support must follow its lead in matters of legislative tactics and in voting for speaker of the House. An MCCL-supported candidate is expected to refrain from publicly supporting any elected official or candidate whom the MCCL considers "pro-abortion." (The terminology here is politically disputed. Those who favor outlawing abortion call themselves "pro-life" and label their opponents "pro-abortion." The latter call themselves "pro-choice" and label their opponents "anti-choice." In this narrative I call each group what it calls itself.) Democratic candidates who give the MCCL everything it demands on the abortion issue, for instance, are intensely pressured at public forums to go the further step of publicly refusing to support the party's national and statewide candidates, and often enough in my district Democratic candidates have capitulated to this pressure. We will see later in the story how this tactic came into play in my own campaign.

The local Democratic Party had been bitterly divided over the abortion issue in the decade preceding my election as chair. Pro-life activists had been far more successful locally than their opponents in mobilizing supporters to attend precinct caucuses, pass pro-life resolutions, and elect local party officers. Of the self-identified pro-lifers who attended Democratic caucuses, some had no attachment to the Democratic Party whatsoever but cared only about one issue; others were willing to support and work for only those Democratic candidates whom they considered pro-life; still others — among them social justice-oriented Catholics — were genuinely torn between their conscientious opposition to abortion and their support for the Democratic platform on issues such as education, health care, workers' rights, and environmental protection.

Those local Democrats who held pro-choice views on the abortion issue were usually willing to support pro-life Democrats who had won party endorsement. In this respect the pro-choice local Democrats were more willing to compromise than their counterparts on the other side of the issue. (Pro-choicers' willingness to compromise was a district-specific phenomenon. In Twin Cities districts pro-choice activists could be as single-issue as the MCCL.) And many other local Democrats — perhaps most — considered the abortion issue less important than other problems and lamented the tragic divisions it had produced in the party. But lamenting the divisions did not make them disappear. Such was the fractured local party I inherited upon being elected chair.

There was at least one promising result of the 1990 caucuses that favored my efforts as chair to build an effective local Democratic party. In 1990, and again in 1992, an unusually large number of caucus attendees identified themselves with organized labor. Many of these worked at the Champion International paper mill in Sartell, the largest employer in the district, and the scene of some fierce contract disputes at the time. (The Sartell mill under new ownership is today Verso Paper.) In rural Stearns County organized labor had been relatively weak and in previous years not strongly motivated to attend caucus. But the labor dispute at Champion, together with the increasingly common statewide and nationwide practice by employers of hiring "permanent replacements" for striking workers, drove many union-affiliated workers to become active in local party politics in the same year that I first attended caucus and ended up as party chair.[10]

The labor-identified local Democrats, and especially the ones who worked at Champion, turned out to be among the most committed and effective supporters of my efforts as chair from 1990 to 1992 to build a local party — and they continued to be among my best campaign volunteers when I myself ran for office in 1992. Even though a specific set of issues had initially spurred them to attend caucus, many of them soon showed an interest in a wider range of issues and genuinely *learned* from their participation in politics. This distinguished them from the "single-issue" participants on the abortion question that had so divided the party. Whatever their views on the abortion question (they were divided on this like the rest of us), their principal commitment was to bread-and-butter issues: workers' rights, decent wages, quality public education, affordable health care.

I should also add that the Champion people were extremely effective at carrying out the routine but essential work of campaigns: making and placing signs, getting mailings out, organizing parade volunteers, raising money, distributing literature. They were also fun to be around, which counts for a lot when everyone is engaged in time-consuming, often boring work for zero pay.

The same convention that elected me local party chair selected me as delegate to the Democratic state and congressional district conventions, and I took my responsibilities as an initially uncommitted delegate seriously. One of the advantages of Minnesota's caucus system is that it enables ordinary citizens to gather information about candidates through this kind of intense, reciprocal exchange with the candidate in person, instead of depending entirely on the candidates' own advertising and mailings. When Paul Wellstone, who that year challenged and ultimately defeated incumbent Rudy Boschwitz, called me to ask for my vote at the state convention, I kept him on the phone for forty-five minutes. I was skeptical at first of his prospects for winning, but this phone conversation won me over. He remarked during that conversation that for the ordinary citizen, "Washington, D.C., is as far away as Pluto," and he hoped to bridge that distance. I was later to discover that for many citizens in my district, St. Paul was as distant as Pluto.

Searching for a Candidate

I threw myself into my party chair duties with enthusiasm for a new adventure. I organized fund-raisers, quickly taking the local party from bankrupt to well-funded, held regular meetings (an innovation), started up a monthly newsletter, began filling the many vacant precinct chair positions with warm bodies, and set about to learn the character (and restaurants) of the various towns in the district.

I did what I could for our 1990 legislative candidate, Michael (Mitch) Fiedler, who was challenging the Republican incumbent Bernie Omann. It was the labor dispute at the Champion paper mill that motivated Mitch Fiedler to declare himself a candidate. He had been the union president at Champion during the fierce contract dispute, and he ran for the legislature as a way of publicizing the union's side of the story. This meant he had some reason to run for office despite the probability of defeat. Voters typically take it for granted that they will have choices in an election contest. But in fact throughout the United States a significant and growing percentage of state legislative elections — and in some states a majority of legislative elections — are literally unopposed.[11] Anyone who has ever tried to recruit candidates to run against well-settled incumbents knows how difficult and unnatural it is for human beings to put themselves through a time-consuming and reputation-risking campaign with no realistic chance of winning. When someone does run against great odds, it is often because he or she has "something to say," and this was the case with Mitch.

Bernie Omann had succeeded his father in the office. In 1988 Omann won 59 percent to 41 percent against Jay Klaphake, a stronger Democratic candidate than we were fielding in 1990. Mitch himself did not campaign effectively and in the 1990 election received only 32 percent of the vote to Omann's 68 percent. But Mitch had made his point, and as party chair I was grateful to him for sparing us the embarrassment of allowing Omann to run unopposed. (Both Fiedler and Klaphake had declared themselves 100 percent pro-life, but so was Omann. So this issue had little effect on the 1988 and 1990 campaigns.) No other Democrat entered the 16A race in 1990 or, so far as I know, even gave it a thought.

By December 1990 I was pleased with this new adventure in political participation but also drained and ready to move on to other things. I had been awarded a full-year fellowship with the Program on Constitutional Government at Harvard University. Because I was going to be away for most of 1991, I invited the local party to replace me as chair. The other party officers insisted this was unnecessary because party chairs did not do much in nonelection years, and I would be back in time to organize the precinct caucuses in March 1992.

So off I went to Cambridge, Massachusetts, still officially chair of District 16 DFL in central Minnesota but far away, breathing the intellectual air of the late eighteenth century, my mind filled for most of the next year with James Madison, Alexander Hamilton, Thomas Jefferson, and other characters and arguments of that distant age. The campaign to ratify the

U.S. Constitution in 1787–88 seemed much closer and more vivid to me than any campaign back in Minnesota.

Yet I did return to Minnesota during the summer months of 1991, and this kept alive a sense of party-chair duty that was otherwise far from my mind that year. My most fateful act of summer 1991 was to form a search committee to recruit potential candidates to run against Bernie Omann in 1992. Jim Graeve, a longtime local Democratic activist, agreed to chair the search committee so that its work could continue when I returned to Cambridge for fall semester of 1991.

All of the local Democratic activists considered it extremely important to field a credible candidate in 1992 for the 16A legislative seat (which became 14A after redistricting). It was not simply a matter of winning the seat; we all recognized that was a long shot even with a strong candidate. But fielding a strong candidate would prove that our local party-rebuilding efforts had borne fruit, and this in turn would boost Democratic congressional, gubernatorial, senatorial, and presidential campaigns in our region. Conversely the embarrassment of failing to recruit a local candidate at all (even a mere name on the ballot) would indicate that all of our party-building efforts had been in vain: all dressed up and nowhere to go. My department colleague Kay Wolsborn, who studies and teaches about political parties, remarked to me: "You *have* to have a candidate."

The search committee met several times during summer 1991, and a few more times in my absence in the fall. We discussed the characteristics we sought in a candidate. We wanted a longtime resident deeply rooted in the district and locally respected, perhaps a school board or city council member. A dairy farmer would be good symbolism. Other things being equal, we preferred someone from an old and large Stearns County family who had dozens of relatives still living in the district. We wanted a candidate who would campaign vigorously door-to-door, not just someone who would merely show up at the occasional parade or picnic. We wanted someone who would not run away from the rest of the Democratic ticket as the Bertram brothers did.

We agreed from the outset that we would endorse and work for a credible candidate whatever position he or she took on the abortion issue so long as the individual genuinely supported the Democratic agenda on bread-and-butter issues. If anything, our group of local activists, many of whom were pro-choice in their personal views, leaned toward recruiting a pro-life Democrat because we felt a pro-choice candidate had no chance here.

Our discussion of preferred characteristics went fine. We failed, however, to draw out any actual candidates, despite diligent efforts at persuasion. It got to the point where we would begin search committee meetings by declaring, only half-jokingly, "No one gets out of this room until we have a candidate." I explained that I did not consider myself a credible candidate and did not intend to run. I was not pro-life by the standards of the district; that was reason enough in itself. Besides, I was a very recent transplant with no family roots and no community involvements other than serving as party chair.

Moreover my own personal and professional goals seemed irreconcilable with the time demands of running for office. I wanted to establish myself as a political theorist and scholar of American political thought. This would require an enormous commitment of time on top of my teaching duties. I was still untenured, and I would need to demonstrate excellence as a teacher; the time and energy cost of a legislative campaign could interfere with this. I was willing to do my duty as party chair, a time-demanding job in itself, and work to recruit credible candidates, but I felt that was the limit of my obligation.

Everyone else on the search committee also explained why he or she was unwilling to be a candidate. My excuses were no better or worse than anyone else's. I returned to Harvard and the intellectual air of the eighteenth century and completely forgot about my party duties until I returned to Minnesota in January 1992. As party chair I was principally responsible for organizing our district's precinct caucuses scheduled for March 3. This being a presidential election year, caucuses would be especially important. And thinking about the caucuses reminded me that we still lacked a candidate.

Sleepless Nights

My wife and I lived in the Meadowlark Apartments on the eastern edge of St. Joseph. One night in mid-February I was tossing and turning all night and keeping Pia awake. She asked me why I couldn't sleep. I hesitated for several minutes and then told her: I was thinking about running. She then told me the same thought had crossed her mind. It was about three or four in the morning. We decided if we couldn't sleep anyway, we might as well get up and talk about it.

Part of the motivation was the embarrassment of not yet having a candidate. But duty to the party alone does not explain it. The truth was that without being aware of it I had been sliding in this direction for two years. I had invested my work as party chair with a degree of passion and energy that far exceeded the modest duties of the position. This was evident to others in the party long before I recognized it myself.

Part of it, too, was my own evolution as a political scientist and teacher. I now realized that the attitude of the detached observer of politics that I had assumed all the way through college and graduate school was sterile. The theorists I studied and wrote about had not remained detached from politics; why should I? I encouraged my students to become active in politics; why shouldn't I take my own advice? My two years' participation in local politics made me ashamed to realize how little I had known about politics before. Win or lose, I would in the end have a clearer understanding of this thing "politics," to which I had devoted my professional life. Running for office could be a natural extension of my teaching and a continuation of my own education, if I campaigned in the right way.

Pia and I were in perfect agreement on one thing: that if I was going to do this, I would run to win. I was not just going to put my name on the ballot. We were realistic about my slim chances of knocking off a Republican incumbent in a Republican district on a first attempt. But we knew I could do better than 32 percent of the vote. And in the process we would say and do things that had never been said and done by a candidate in this district before.

We knew the abortion issue was our greatest problem. We got knots in our stomachs every time we thought about this. I suspect that many people in the opponent's camp believed we did not know what we were getting into. But we did.

I had never been any kind of pro-choice activist, and I do not think I have ever used that label to describe my views. Like most Americans, I am internally torn on this matter, and I have always been especially uneasy with middle- and late-term abortions. If I had been running for office in the Twin Cities or their suburbs, my views would probably have been labeled "pro-life" by opponents courting the pro-choice vote. But running for legislature in rural Stearns and Morrison counties—in MCCL territory—was a different matter altogether. Here it was all or nothing. Either you were "100 percent pro-life," or you were an enemy. This was partly a matter of doctrine (to be "pro-life" meant supporting the prohibition of all abortions) and partly a matter of sustaining the organization's political monopoly in the district: to be pro-life meant that in one's campaigning and legislating one would defer to the MCCL's judgment on all matters the organization considered important.

I considered an absolute ban on abortion both unjust and unenforceable, and I had no intention of taking marching orders from any organization. Moreover it would have been shameful to try to win office by publicly voicing a view that contradicted what I had expressed in private conversations with friends and colleagues over the years. I would not win office if it meant looking like a prostitute to those who knew me best. I had a job; I did not need the legislative seat that badly. I also knew from polls and from my own political organizing that my own views on abortion were not far out of line with the community.

Once my candidacy became public knowledge, I had dozens of conversations with Democratic legislators and political activists who were used to campaigning in pro-choice leaning districts where the MCCL is weak and where many Republicans also run as pro-choice candidates. In many cases their advice was something like this: "Just say whatever you need to say to win. Tell them you are 'pro-life' and leave it at that." What lay behind such advice was, first, the assumption that rural Stearns County was so locked in the antiabortion camp that there was nothing to be gained by heroic gestures; and second, the condescending assumption that I could say the opposite of what I really thought and none of the locals would suspect it. It was unlikely that I could fool the pro-lifers into voting for me by mistake.

I decided instead to attempt some morally coherent middle position on the abortion issue. I would support greater restrictions on middle- and late-term abortions but leave abortion unrestricted in the first trimester of pregnancy. I would concede that abortion was bad and that its numbers should be reduced but argue that persuasion and education were more effective in this regard than coercion. I would signal my willingness to engage in dialogue with activists on both sides about how best to reduce the number of abortions that occur in the United States. Pia and I condensed these ideas into a written statement that we titled "The Abortion Controversy: A Search for Common Ground" (see chapter 5 of this narrative).

It would be misleading to say that I "campaigned on" the abortion issue. My principal campaign themes were to become "health care," "jobs and taxes," "education," and "environment." But the abortion issue would inevitably come up, and I had to have an answer. I consistently refused to allow myself to be labeled either "pro-choice" or "pro-life" and instead insisted that people respond to what I was saying rather than force me into rigid, preexisting categories.

Once Pia and I had decided to explore the possibility of my running, we began sketching out a campaign strategy. Pia agreed that if I ran, she would manage the campaign. At the time Pia had a term contract teaching position at St. Benedict's and St. John's. We had met in college at the University of Chicago, where we were both political science majors. After college she served three years in the Peace Corps in Swaziland in southern Africa, teaching secondary mathematics and setting up an agricultural cooperative. She returned to the United States and completed a master's degree from the Fletcher School of Law and Diplomacy. We married in July 1988 and moved to Minnesota in fall 1988 when I began my teaching duties. Her Peace Corps experience and graduate degree pointed her in the direction of some kind of international or foreign-service career. But there was not much work of that kind available in Stearns County. By 1992 she was ready for a new challenge, and once we made the decision, she threw herself into this project with a passion equal to my own. Given the enormous time commitment we knew this would involve, we would have seen little of each other if she had not managed the campaign.

Before I made any final decision, I sounded out local party activists whose judgment I trusted: Jim Graeve, Becky Hooper, Kurt Rasmussen, Dennis Molitor, Jack and Melissa Kitzmiller, and a few others. I wanted to know not simply whether they would support me if I ran (this was not in doubt), but whether they genuinely believed I was a strong candidate. I also wanted to make sure my backers knew where I stood on the abortion issue. In several of these phone conversations the person I was sounding out said to me something like this: "People are tired of being bullied on abortion. They are sick of both sides. They want to hear about other issues."

I also called John Brandl, a professor at the University of Minnesota's Humphrey Institute and St. John's alumnus who had served ten years in the Minnesota Senate. Despite his association with a quantitatively heavy public policy school, John—both as legislator and as scholar—has always been especially concerned with the moral dimensions of politics. John was impressed by my approach to the abortion issue: he believed it was both courageous and morally and politically right, not only for the district I was running in but for the state and nation as a whole. He strongly encouraged me to go forward.

At the time I was making these exploratory phone calls, in my role as party chair I continued to search for other candidates willing to run. I was still ready to step aside for a better candidate. I issued two or three more invitations to other potential candidates. I had no takers, and this reinforced my own determination.

As a courtesy I called my associate chair, Alice Schreifels, who was an active MCCL member. We had worked well together as chair and cochair in organizing the caucuses. I told her I was thinking about running. There was a long pause that suggested she knew what was coming next. I laid out my position on abortion. She said, "Jim, you know I can't support you." I told her I understood; I just felt I owed it to her to tell her myself before it became public.

I knew I had to call Joe and Jeff Bertram. It would be impossible to win if they were publicly working against me. I had been on good if somewhat distant terms with both Bertrams in my work as party chair. In my phone conversations with them I made clear where I stood on abortion so they could decide then whether to support me or keep their distance. Joe Bertram (the state senator, half of whose district coincided with the one I would be running in) was noncommittal but friendly enough that I concluded he would not be out there working against me. Jeff Bertram said he would support me. This was a good sign. Given the intensity of the abortion issue, Jeff would not have taken the risk of supporting me if he had not judged me to be a competitive candidate.

One phone conversation, however, shook my determination to the core and led Pia and me to reconsider not only whether I should run for office, but whether we should even continue to live in Stearns County. I had called Andy Blauvelt, a fellow political scientist and colleague who had been active in Minnesota politics for years. In 1990 he had worked on Paul Wellstone's U.S. Senate campaign, and over the years on many other legislative and congressional campaigns. Andy knew Minnesota politics through and through. When I told him I was seriously considering running and explained my position on the abortion issue, he said, "Do *not* do this. You have no idea how powerful the MCCL is in this district. There is not another district in the state, probably not another district in the whole United States, that would be more difficult for someone like you to win." I told him I knew my chances of winning were not high on a first run, but I was willing to do it anyway. He was relentless. "It's not just that you will lose. You will get crushed, and it will be emotionally devastating." He added, "You have no idea what the MCCL can do to you. They will go after you teaching at a Catholic college, and it could endanger your job." I told him that we did not have a candidate, and we had to have one. "There is still time for a candidate who fits the district to come out," he replied. "But if you get in there, you will drive out other candidates, and the result will be a disaster for both you and the party."

The course of the campaign was to show that Andy's warnings were not unfounded. I would learn firsthand about the extraordinarily intimidating pressure that the MCCL and its allies can put on candidates. And the potential threat to my position as an untenured faculty member at a Catholic university was not out of the question. I have seen elsewhere how religiously affiliated universities often become the target of intense political pressure from off-campus groups, who can damage the university's standing among its contributors and natural recruiting base. Later, when I was campaigning door-to-door, I encountered a number of anti-abortion activists who, rather than engaging me in argument, simply said, "I can't believe they let you teach there." Late in the campaign, as we will see, some not-subtle hints of the same type were included in a radio ad directed against me. Andy was not making any of this up.

I reported this conversation to Pia, and it led us into a period of wrenching, paralyzing doubt. We both knew Andy and respected his judgment.

We also had observed enough from our two years' experience in Stearns County politics to know what Andy was talking about. His predictions had the effect of reigniting all the doubts and fears that we had been suppressing for the past two weeks.

We had another long, completely sleepless night. The lack of sleep probably contributed to the peculiar character of our reasoning. At three in the morning we were ready not only to call off the idea of my running for office but also to pull up stakes and move away somewhere — anywhere. "If we can't publicly say what we believe, we shouldn't be living here," we repeated to one another. We felt ourselves to be aliens in a community that neither understood us nor wanted us. All of our political participation and political organizing of the past two years suddenly appeared to us a self-deceptive game: the community was polite to our faces but laughing behind our backs. We would refuse to live in a community that did not accept us as full members. By four in the morning we were making plans to put ourselves on the job market and move away.

By seven in the morning (still without a minute of sleep) this same overwrought state of mind had deflected our reasoning in the opposite direction. "This is crazy," we said to each other. "We are not going to live in fear. We have as much right to live here as anyone else does." In the early morning light, moving away seemed cowardly and shameful. For the very same reasons, my not running for office because of the abortion issue seemed cowardly and shameful. It was a reflection of our peculiar sleepless state of mind that running for office or moving away seemed the only two courses of action open to us. We came to the irrevocable conclusion that I had to run for office.

By the time of the 1992 precinct caucuses on Tuesday, March 3, I had communicated my decision to all the party officers and precinct chairs in the local Democratic Party. On Friday, March 27, the *St. Cloud Times* reported that I had announced my candidacy. On March 28 I made my first public speech as a candidate at the Stearns 14 County convention and spoke again at the Morrison County convention the next week. On April 29 I was endorsed without opposition at the Senate District 14 Democratic convention. I held my first fund-raiser that day with Dee Long, the speaker of the Minnesota House, as special guest. I began door-knocking in St. Joseph on April 30.

On May 2 the incumbent I was challenging, Bernie Omann, was endorsed by his party to run for the seventh congressional district seat against Democrat Collin Peterson. My luck had turned. I was now running for an open seat. It would still be an uphill battle, given the character of the district and my status as an outsider, but my odds had improved. Any number of Democratic candidates, including some who had refused my invitation to run, would have jumped in if they had known ahead of time it would be an open seat. But my six-week head start and willingness to take on an incumbent gave me an unassailable position within the party. No other Democratic candidate ever filed. And that was fine with me. By now I was thrilled to be running for the Minnesota House of Representatives.

Planning a Campaign

There was only one way I could hope to win this election: one vote at a time. I did not have any family roots or local reputation to give me a boost. I had to meet as many voters as I could, engage them in conversation, and persuade them to vote for me.

This in turn determined our campaign strategy. It had to be from beginning to end a door-knocking campaign. And as much as possible it had to be me in person at the door, at least once and preferably twice. Door knocking by campaign volunteers had to be in addition to—not in place of—my own visits. Everything else on which we spent time or money—parades, mailings, literature drops, group door-knocks, radio and print ads, lawn signs—would have to function to reinforce the (hopefully positive) impression I made in person.

I had no family ties in the district (my last name broadcast this fact), had no children in schools, did not belong to a church, and with the exception of serving as party chair, had no community involvements. The only organized political network of any significance in the district, the MCCL, was guaranteed to be on my opponent's side and fiercely opposed to me. A Republican, pro-life candidate might win a Republican, pro-life district without much door knocking; as a Democratic candidate in a Republican district I could not hope to win in any other way.

My one advantage was that once Bernie Omann announced he was running for Congress, I knew I could out-door-knock any opponent. I started door-knocking on April 30. My eventual opponent did not publicly announce until June 16 and was not endorsed by his party until July 7.[12] Even if my opponent had attempted to match my door-knocking rate (which he did not), I had had at least a nine-week head start.

We knew it would be impossible for me to meet and speak personally with every voter. Our goal was that I meet and speak with the majority of likely voters in the district. This was within the realm of possibility, but both the numbers and the logistics of distance and time were daunting.

There were approximately 22,000 people of voting age living in the district, residing in about 10,000 households. If I began the first week of May and door-knocked 6 days a week, I would have 144 door-knocking days. If on each door-knocking day I visited 50 households, the total for a six-month campaign would be 7,200 households—a solid majority of the total. I could, and in fact did, push that number higher by sometimes door-knocking 7 days a week and by sometimes getting to 60 or 70 houses in a day rather than 50.

But these apparently straightforward figures were complicated by a number of factors. On average about a third of the households had no one home (or no one willing to answer the door). The at-home rate varied depending on time of day and whether it was a weekday or weekend. A brochure left on the door with the handwritten note "sorry I missed you" is better than nothing at all but far inferior to an actual contact.

A second challenge was distance and driving time. There were thirteen cities in the district: from largest to smallest in voting age population, they were Sartell (eighteen-and-older population of 3,574 and growing rapidly), St. Joseph (1,686), Albany (1,155), Avon (666), Royalton (521), Holdingford (392), Rice (385), St. Stephen (380), Upsala (280), Bowlus (177), Elmdale (89), Pleasant Lake (57), and St. Anthony (47). District 14A also included the following townships: in Stearns County, Albany, Brockway, Holding, Krain, Le Sauk, St. Joseph, and St. Wendel; in Morrison County, Bellevue, Elmdale, Swan River, and Two Rivers. The district also included two fragments of Benton County, across the Mississippi River: Rice and the east part of Sartell.

In Sartell and St. Joseph, the two largest cities, it was easy enough to get to fifty households in two hours, even allowing time for several unrushed

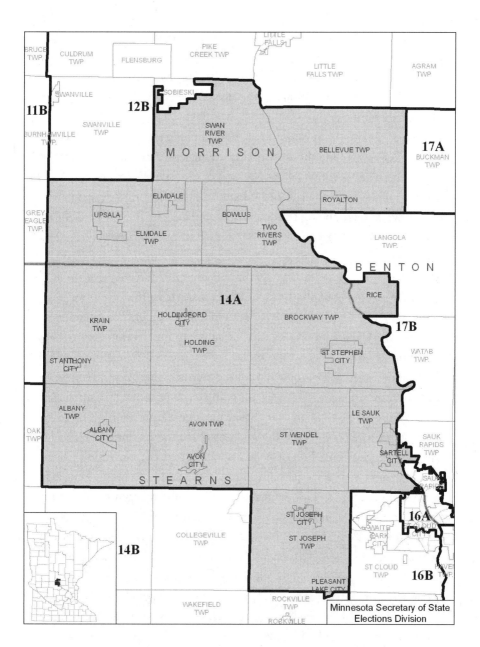

Minnesota House District 14A in 1992

conversations. But for small cities like St. Anthony (voting age population: forty-seven) far from my home, driving time there and back greatly exceeded door-knocking time. From St. Joseph, where I lived, it was an hour's driving time to Upsala at the northwest corner of the district in Morrison County.

Moreover the great majority of households in the district were not located in towns but in the surrounding townships. Thus, for instance, the city of Avon had a voting age population of 666, while surrounding Avon Township had 2,675; the city of Holdingford had a voting age population of 392, while surrounding Holding Township had 739; the city of Elmdale had 89, and Elmdale Township, 551. This distribution between city and township was typical in most of the district. In an area consisting principally of farms or former farms with still occupied farmhouses, it could take six hours to get to fifty households. In many townships the voting age population was large but located in scattered developments of fifteen or so houses, with significant driving time in between one development pocket and another. If I had been running for legislature in Minneapolis, I could easily have visited every single household at least twice over the course of a six-month campaign. That was not going to be possible in District 14A.

A further complication was that it made sense to door-knock some places twice, even if it meant I would not get to some others at all. By far the most powerful method of persuasion was to meet someone at his or her doorstep twice, once perhaps in July and again in October, especially if my opponent had not been there at all. Our campaign plan was for me to door-knock every town twice and each township, or as much of a township as I could get to, once. I would finish all the towns over the summer and door-knock them a second time in September and October. My door-knocking notes indicate that I was far more successful on that second visit in getting individuals to promise to vote for me. But given time constraints, for every house in a town I visited twice, there was some house or farm I would not get to at all.

In most of the district's cities and townships the number of registered voters was close to the number of adults of voting age, indicating an older and settled population. But there were fast-growing areas like the city of

Sartell and St. Wendel, Le Sauk, and Avon townships with many new residents not yet registered to vote. In St. Joseph a large number of college students would be eligible to vote for the first time.

To the logistical challenges of a door-knocking campaign must be added the other demands on my time. When I began door-knocking in May, I was still teaching three classes. I had the summer months free but would be back to full-time teaching from Labor Day on through election day; Pia was also teaching. Both of us would be doing the equivalent of two full-time jobs seven days a week.

We laid out a demanding schedule and kept to it. My June 15 campaign progress report noted that I had already been to fifteen hundred households; by August 12, I reported having visited more than four thousand households. This kind of pace surprises people who have never done it. I was campaigning one Sunday afternoon during the summer and encountered one of my university colleagues. "Do you do this every weekend?" he asked. "Yes," I replied, "and every weekday also."

The Opponent

By the end of June the contest had become a two-man race. I had no opposition at the endorsing convention or in the primary. My opponent defeated another candidate at the Republican endorsing convention in June and had no primary challenger. Who I ultimately became as a candidate was in part a reflection of who my opponent was and vice versa.

The best introduction to my opponent, Steve Dehler, and the nature of his campaign is his own introductory statement at the St. Joseph candidate forum on October 6, where he reiterated what had been his campaign theme all along.

"I'm Steve Dehler. I was born near St. Wendel, and I grew up on several farms, one around Holdingford and one around Long Prairie. . . . My mother grew up around Brooten and Sedan, and my father grew up around Putnam in Morrison County. I've been married to Jean Linnemann since 1972 and I have two daughters. . . . This election gives you a distinct choice between two candidates. Growing up in this district gives me a unique insight into knowing the people that I represent. Community involvement has given me the insight to know how much volunteer effort goes into making the small communities and District 14A what they are."[13]

Dehler must have appeared a much stronger candidate for this district than I was. He was forty-two years old and had lived in the area since before I was born. He was completing his first term as mayor of St. Joseph, the second-largest city in the district. Before that he had served eighteen years on the city council. He was from one old central Minnesota family and had married into another: his wife's family, the Linnemanns, was one of the founding families of St. Joseph and had operated a general store that was long a fixture of the town. Dehler had all the community involvements I lacked: Jaycees, Chamber of Commerce, Knights of Columbus, lector and parish council at church, stage manager of a ballet company, member of the St. Joe / Cold Spring Medical Planning Council, among other things. (I document this from a campaign mailing he sent out that listed all of his community involvements on one side of the page and a big blank under my name on the other side of the page.)

He had the advantage of being a Republican in a Republican district (Bernie Omann sent around to the district a letter endorsing Dehler as his successor). He was not a dairy farmer, but he had at least worked summer jobs on farms, which was more than I could claim. His wife worked for food services at the College of St. Benedict, in the same building that housed my office, and his daughter was a student at the college. Strategically one could assume that his position in St. Joseph, the only reliably Democratic town in the district, and his links to the college would offset the only advantages I possessed, while his family roots, community involvements, and partisan affiliation would give him a clear advantage everywhere else.

Personally he was genial and hard to dislike. When he and I encountered each other on the campaign trail, our meetings were always good-humored and decent, and we occasionally swapped campaign stories. We had both pledged from the outset that this would not be a nasty campaign, and except for a radio ad he signed off on late in the campaign and my response (see chapter 5), we honored that commitment. With our living in the same town and my crossing paths with him or members of his family nearly every day, it would have been counterproductive and disruptive to the community to conduct vicious campaigns even if we had been disposed to do so. And we were so different, in personality, life history, and on issues, that a bitter campaign would have been beside the point. Candidates sometimes resort to campaign strategies of personal attack when they believe there is no better way to distinguish themselves from their opponent in voters' minds. There was no such need in our case.

On the abortion issue he was straightforward and clear. "Life begins at conception and choice ends at conception," he repeated at every stage of the campaign. He did not make exceptions in the case of rape and incest. In the St. Joseph candidate forum, in response to a follow-up question critical of his position on rape and incest, he asserted that "I can't believe that anybody who lets their child come to full term will not love it." There was no question who would have the support of the MCCL in this election. Over the years I have seen more than one candidate pander on the abortion issue. But I think Dehler was speaking from religious conviction. On the other principal conservative hot-button issue, Dehler gave the National Rifle Association everything it wanted and had their clear support also. With respect to health care, which was a central campaign theme for me, Dehler insisted at the debate and throughout the campaign that "free enterprise is a great system" and we should not let government interfere with it.

Alongside these and other self-explanatory conservative positions, Dehler had some ideas of his own that can perhaps be described as unique. He favored automatic capital punishment for everyone convicted of murder. On the term limits issue he told the *St. Joseph Newsleader* (June 19, 1992) that "he favors an 8–10 year term of office with no successive re-election for politicians at all levels of government and an eight-year, single term limit for the President of the United States." He believed that having a congressional election every two years was "an unbelievable waste of money." (He meant a single term of eight to ten years for all elected officials, not a ten-year accumulated limit on shorter terms.)

He did have some vulnerabilities as a candidate, but fewer obvious ones than I had. His two-year record as mayor of St. Joseph had received mixed reviews, resulting from a number of local controversies with which I never had to involve myself. Linnemann's store, the old family business, had under his ownership recently succumbed to the pressures facing many small grocery stores and gone out of business. He was looking around for new entrepreneurial ventures and in the meantime had one part-time job at a convenience store and another as a dispatcher for the Morrison County Jail. Many people speculated that he was running for the legislature because he needed a full-time job.

Early in his campaign he sent around a letter to prospective supporters inviting them to help him "visit every house in the district." So he seems likewise to have intended his to be a door-knocking campaign, and as the campaign went on, he must have been getting pressure from Republican activists to meet my challenge in this respect. As it turned out, though I know he did some door-knocking (I once encountered him door-knocking in Avon near the house where I now live), he never personally got to nearly as many doors as I did. Whether this was due to lack of time, an underestimation of my strength as a candidate, or some other reason, I cannot say.

Volunteers

Running for public office is in one sense always a lonely affair, because no matter what others can do or say for you, it is your name on the ballot and your reputation on the line. No effective campaign is an individual effort, however, but instead depends on the dedication and energy of dozens of volunteers.

The only way I could free up enough time for an ambitious door-knocking schedule was to have volunteers doing everything that did not need to be done by the candidate. Every hour a candidate spends calling volunteers to work a parade, pounding in stakes for a lawn sign, picking up brochures from the printers, filling out campaign expenditure reports, arranging who will bring potato salad to the campaign picnic, and so on is an hour lost to meeting voters. (I have observed more than one legislative campaign where the candidate was doing all these things.)

In my campaign, everyone was doing their campaign work without pay and often at the sacrifice of precious weekend and family time. Volunteers have to believe in you, both as a candidate and as a human being: their commitment is to you personally. You in turn have an obligation to make the activity worth their time, win or lose. It is also essential to make the campaign effort itself a social community, with its own stories, in-jokes, and new friendships, because this partly compensates for the ordinary social life individuals are sacrificing to work on the campaign. I also depended on campaign volunteers to educate me about issues and the characteristics and needs of the communities they lived in. It is impossible for me to do justice to all the individual volunteers who generously gave their time and whose belief in me reinforced my own belief in myself. I offer the following abbreviated list with apologies and thanks to all the others.

Jim Graeve, a social worker, was a DFL political activist from years back and had once worked as a staffer for Congressman Rick Nolan and participated in protests against the Vietnam War. He had more campaign experience than all the rest of us put together. He knew the difference between a strong candidate and a weak one, and I would not have run if Jim had not judged me to be a strong candidate.

Becky Hooper worked for Stearns County Social Services and was a key source of information on issues related to care for the elderly—for demographic reasons an especially important issue in the district. She lived just outside the boundaries of the district and so could not vote for me. She compensated for that disability with tireless campaign work and by keeping us laughing when we needed it most.

Ellen Wahlstrom, more active in retirement than most people are at any time in their lives, did campaign work almost every day. Her tireless phoning ensured that there were abundant volunteers at every campaign event.

Kurt Rasmussen, one of my campaign cochairs, worked at the Champion International paper mill in Sartell and had taught industrial arts in the public schools. He was a key source of information on labor issues. He was a great storyteller (especially about his Boundary Waters canoe trips) and a wizard at making Jim Read yard signs appear along key highways.

Dennis Molitor also worked at Champion and had recently been elected to the Sartell City Council. He was genial and soft-spoken and incredibly effective at persuading people to contribute to my campaign. Without Dennis, I would have had to spend much more of my own time fund-raising.

Jack Kitzmiller, who also worked at Champion, took over as local party chair when I resigned to run for office. He created the first good database our local party ever had and did the same for my campaign. His wife, Melissa, my other campaign cochair, allowed us to use their house for campaign meetings until we could afford to rent an office. She was also my key informant on the needs of the Sartell school system as seen from a parent's perspective.

Bob Spaeth, former dean at St. John's, was our campaign treasurer, the person legally responsible for our compliance with election law. He agreed to be treasurer only if we promised to visit him in jail. He was well informed about Minnesota political history (before his untimely death in 1994, he was collecting materials for a history of the Democratic Farmer-Labor party), and he helped us see our own campaign as a continuation of a great political tradition.

Peg McGlinch was a political science major at the College of St. Benedict. She organized our highly effective get-out-the-vote effort among college students. She spent her Friday and Saturday nights with us at the campaign office instead of hanging out with her peers. "Peg, don't you have a life?" we would ask. But she had discovered her calling. Two years later, while still in college, she managed a legislative campaign, then won the Truman Scholarship (for those intending a career in public service), attended Harvard Law School, and now is an experienced and sought-after staffer on Capitol Hill.

Forward to the Doors

All of this was preparation: studying maps, recruiting volunteers, raising early money, working out positions on issues. There was still one piece missing from the picture: the voter. Unless and until I reached the voter, face-to-face and one at a time, none of this preparation would pay off. So let us move forward to conversations at the door.

CHAPTER TWO

Doorstep Conversations

I march along to the next house, careful not to endanger a vote by cutting across the lawn. I record the street address and the name if visible on the mailbox. On my way up the driveway I look for politically revealing bumper stickers, yard signs, and posters. I carry a handful of campaign brochures and a clipboard (which I try to keep inconspicuous) on which I record each contact's sex, first and last name if they are willing to reveal it, and an estimate of their age. Later I will classify each voter according to his or her response to me: positive, negative, neutral, definitely voting for me, definitely voting against me, probably not voting. If I succeed in engaging the voter in political conversation, I carefully record what he or she said, sometimes in great detail if the individual intrigued me or provided new perspective on issues. If time permits, the next day I will send the voter a handwritten letter referring specifically to our actual conversation.

At the door my opening is always the same: "Hello. My name is Jim Read, and I'm running for state representative in District 14A. I'm here to ask for your vote." You have to ask for their vote, lest they think you are there to hit them up for money or save their soul. And even if they know you want their vote, they still want to be asked.

I then say, "Are there any issues especially important to you, or any questions you would like to ask me?" I don't impose my own views unless invited. My purpose is to draw them into conversation so they will remember my face and name even after the brochure is thrown away. In many cases they say politely, "Not just at the moment," or "I can't think of anything offhand." I hand them my brochure, explaining that it describes me and my views on key issues, direct their attention to my address and phone number, and invite them to call or write me whenever they have a question. I say, "I hope I can count on your vote," thank them for their time, and go on to the next house.

Or we manage some nonpolitical conversation. Upon hearing their name I might ask, "Are you related to —— Ostendorf" [or Schwinghammer, or Pfannenstein, or Salzer] of Holdingford [or St. Anna, or St. Joseph, or St. Wendel Township]?" whom I have already met in the course of my door knocking. In Stearns County the answer to this question was always yes; what varied was how near or distant the kinship. Proving that I had met their relatives and remembered their names was a way of connecting myself with a community in which I had no family roots myself.

Or we talk about heat, cold, humidity, rain or lack of it, a thunderstorm on the horizon. (John Brandl, former dean of the Humphrey Institute and onetime Minnesota legislator, maintains there are two indispensable qualifications for any legislative candidate. One is the physical capacity to get from one door to another. The other is the capacity to discern changes in the weather so you will have something to talk about at the door.) "Will you promise to make it rain?" one voter asked me. I do not remember whether I answered yes or no.

Such encounters might appear superficial. But in-person meetings of this kind—even brief ones—between voter and candidate are essential to a healthy democracy. And for the majority of voters, such conversations are unlikely to occur with candidates for any office higher than state legislator.

Today there are approximately 700,000 inhabitants for every congressional district and far more for the typical U.S. Senate and gubernatorial seat. Communication with voters in campaigns for these offices mostly means *unidirectional* communication: messages produced on one side and consumed on the other. In contrast, when I ran for the Minnesota Legislature, there were approximately 33,000 inhabitants (including children) in each house district. It is possible to meet and converse personally with the majority of the district's eligible voters in the course of a single election campaign if one works hard enough.

No campaign ad, mailing, literature drop, or campaign volunteer visit can take the place of the candidate himself or herself, at the door, saying in effect to each potential voter: "Here I am. That is my name on the ballot. This is your chance to ask me questions or speak your mind." An in-person visit signals accountability. Every voter at the door, however uninformed, understands that message. It is an unspoken subtext even in conversations about the weather or family ties.

Sometimes my appearance at the door with campaign materials in hand would trigger a bitter denunciation of all politicians, but the tone would change when the person realized I was not just another campaign worker. "Well, you showed up yourself. That counts for something," several politician haters told me.

When I succeeded in getting someone to talk politics with me (in about a third of my doorstep meetings), what did they want to talk about? Anything under the sun. Did I think it was fair to use snowmobile licensing fees for purposes other than funding snowmobile trails? What was my opinion of Bill Clinton? Would I promise to get a traffic light on Highway 10 in Royalton (a dangerous intersection)? Would I secure a new elementary school for Sartell? Did I realize that immigrants do not have to pay any taxes at all (a false view I was unable to dislodge)? And, of course, health care costs, taxes, abortion, and guns came up nearly every day. I went to households where I knew I would not get the vote because I felt it was my duty to hear them out; if I were to win, I would have to represent those who voted against me as well as those who supported me.

Many of the people I met had little understanding of Minnesota government or of the difference between federal, state, and local issues. I often found myself playing the role of an itinerant civics teacher for individuals I suspected were unlikely to vote. But I did not consider this a waste of my time. If a candidate at the door asking for their vote does not connect them to the democratic process, who will?

Taking the Plunge

A legislative candidate for whom door knocking is central undergoes a remarkable psychological change over the course of the campaign. At first it feels extremely unnatural to be making unsolicited calls on fifty or more strangers every day to ask for their vote and sound out their political views. It is like plunging from a warm ledge into an ice-cold, fast-moving stream: there is no gradual adjustment—it is all or nothing. You feel at first like an imposter or a home invader. When someone you do not know yells at you angrily or closes the door in your face, you take it personally, and it requires days to recover your emotional balance. Candidates who do not do enough door knocking, who consider it an irritating adjunct to their campaign rather than the centerpiece, typically do not get past this painful and awkward opening stage.

After a month or two of intense door knocking, however, it begins to feel entirely natural: you are now a fish at home in the stream. You realize that most people do not mind the unsolicited call, and many positively welcome it. If you treat what you are doing as natural and necessary, most people will respond in the same spirit. And in the occasional case when someone attacks you, calls you names, treats you as Satan's emissary to Stearns County, you simply say to yourself: "I am probably not going to get this vote. Time to head for the next door." Every doorstep is a fresh beginning.

The longer the campaign goes on, the more you enjoy the door knocking in comparison to everything else that you spend time on. Asking strangers for votes is more enjoyable than asking supporters for money, begging the press to cover your campaign (or responding to distorted coverage), replying to attack ads, meeting with lobbyists who do not care which candidate wins as long as they have access to both, trying to persuade state party operatives your campaign is a competitive one, and attending time-consuming events where you have little chance to speak but it would look bad to be absent. As election day nears, such details and duties take up an increasing percentage of your already scarce time, and yet their actual vote-winning effect is inferior to an equivalent amount of time spent door knocking. By October it was a liberation to get away from all those other tasks and hit the doors.

The standard advice was to spend no more than thirty seconds at a door; some advice said cut it to ten seconds. I myself systematically violated this conventional wisdom, especially in the first four months or so of door knocking. If I believed I could persuade a voter, or if I believed I could learn something valuable from the conversation, I would stay at a single door for fifteen minutes or more and take extensive notes of the conversation. Moreover, I extended the conversations not only with undecideds but even with people I knew would support me anyway and people I knew would vote against me. My door-knocking notes make it clear that many of the conversations I recorded and the observations I made went well beyond the practical goal of securing the individual's vote.

I believed at the time, and still believe, that I was right to draw out the conversations (though there were clearly a few where I stayed too long). I could never forget that I started out the campaign as a complete unknown in a close-knit community, without the family ties and local reputation that make trust easier to secure. I had to create community ties and a reputation in the community in the course of the campaign itself, and ten seconds at the door was not sufficient time to build this kind of capital. I had to rely on the "word of mouth" effect: those who engaged with me in some thoughtful conversation and formed some distinct impression of my character would mention it to others. Someone who had "heard good things about me" from a neighbor or friend might be predisposed in my favor when I showed up at their own door.

Another reason I engaged in extended conversations was that I myself needed to learn quickly about an enormous range of issues I had never considered before, and given time constraints I would learn them faster in door-to-door conversations than any other way. My notes indicate that my longest conversations occurred in the first four months of my door knocking and tended to be on complicated issues on which I myself was struggling to work out a position: for instance, health care reform; addressing the state's projected $800 million budget deficit; educational policy and funding; and the state's expensive and burdensome workers' compensation system, a big issue with small business owners, one to which I had never given a moment's thought before I ran for office.

A final and perhaps most important reason for the extended doorstep conversations was that I would not have been motivated to run for the legislature at all if there had not been something intrinsically interesting about the process, win or lose. I already had a paying job. I was not running for president; were I to win, I would enjoy at best a modest share of political power. If all I had done was spend ten seconds at 7,500 doorsteps, learning nothing, teaching nothing, exchanging nothing, I could not have kept up the pace over six months. And I certainly would not be writing about it fifteen years after the event.

What kept me going was the thrill of discovery. There is no other way to account for how much detail I recorded about human beings, their political hopes and fears, their good and bad ideas, and oddball characteristics. I had found myself in this whole new world of human experience and observation, a hitherto undiscovered universe lying hidden at the end of a thousand ordinary driveways.

My door-knocking notes are my principal source in reconstructing six months of doorstep discourse, my window on the political life of a particular community at a particular moment in time. I estimate that over the course of the campaign I engaged in substantive political conversations (i.e., something beyond chitchat about the weather or some other nonpolitical topic) with more than 2,500 voters living in the district. From a social-scientific perspective my door-knocking records constitute a "database" of respectable size, though of course I was not engaging in an impartial scientific survey. In what follows I draw wherever possible directly from my door-knocking notes. I do not trust myself to improve on the description after the passage of time. My notes record people saying things I could never have invented on my own.

Confronting and Moderating Cynicism

It will surprise no one that in my door knocking I encountered my share of cynics and politician haters. But it may come as a surprise that a personal visit by a candidate sometimes moderates or neutralizes that cynicism.

My first truly nasty encounter came on May 3, the first full week of my door knocking. A colleague from the economics department, Ernie Diedrich, was accompanying me and introducing me to his neighbors in Pleasant Acres, a large housing development north of St. Joseph. (This is an especially effective way to door-knock a neighborhood when you can arrange it.) All encounters that day were friendly, with one exception. One man in his sixties, upon realizing that I was a candidate for office, immediately shouted: "Hit the fucking road!" I was more than willing to take the hint. Unfortunately, Ernie mistakenly thought the man had said, "*Fix* the fucking road," and began talking about the state highway budget, so the hostile encounter was drawn out even further.

Rather than being scarred by this kind of response, it intrigued me and led me systematically to record anti-politician remarks aimed at me over the course of the campaign. Here are some examples:

"Says he hates politicians so much he doesn't want to talk."

"Says he doesn't vote, doesn't trust politicians."

"You guys should all have holes shot in your heads."

"Just keep going—I don't care what you're here for."

"Doesn't like politicians, says they should be sprayed with DDT."

"Wouldn't give name, hates politicians, favors national health care" (here displaying cognitive dissonance).

"You politicians are all crooked."

"You politicians are all a bunch of shitheads."

"Asked if I would work or just take a paycheck."

"You'll turn rotten like all the others."

"Has lost all respect for politicians. Nothing will pass unless the green stuff flows."

"Asked if I had any experience bouncing checks" (referring to the congressional check-bouncing scandal of the moment).

"Confusion about where he is supposed to vote. He will punish them by not voting."

Sometimes I was too hurried or tired to record such remarks in their full splendor. In dozens of cases I simply noted: "Much anger, no clear focus." Rarely did politician haters supply specific reasons; their animosity was expressed in the manner of a self-evident truth.

But for every anti-politician remark of the type noted above, I received remarks of the following kind. These too originate in a basic cynicism about politics. But they show how it can be turned around when a candidate, contrary to an individual's expectations, makes a personal call and demonstrates a willingness to listen and be held accountable.

"Appreciated my coming to the door instead of just dropping literature. Cynical about politicians. Doesn't want me to make any promises."

"Appreciated my coming out here — not many candidates do" (this was in rural Le Sauk Township).

"Said I was the first candidate they'd seen out here."

"Said I was the first candidate who had ever stopped and talked for a while."

"Impressed with the amount of work it took to run for office."

"Thought anyone who'd do the work of going door-to-door was a worthy candidate."

"Impressed that I was 'pounding the pavement' myself."

"Impressed that I would visit in person."

"Impressed that I was door-knocking on a Friday night. I think he'll vote for me."

"Likes my going door-to-door. *Hates* windshield wiper literature" (here referring to the tactic of leafleting church parking lots during services).

"Impressed with my going door-to-door and talking."

"Liked the fact that I was out working."

Remarks of this kind reveal, in the first instance, respect for an individual candidate (especially respect for hard work), not necessarily a changed view of all politicians. But if you are the first candidate for office a politician hater has actually met, or the first who comes off as trustworthy, this might lead them to rethink their own connection to political life as a whole. Perhaps the deepest root of political cynicism is the suspicion that individuals are powerless because politicians do not listen. A door-knocking candidate who, contrary to expectation, clearly does listen plants a new seed that might live past the immediate election season.

The Politically Clueless

The politician haters usually identified themselves quickly and as a result did not take up much of my time. This was not always the case with another group of troublesome contacts: the politically clueless, who would seem to be interested and listen politely until some chance remark revealed the extent of their ignorance or disconnection from politics.

In the first few weeks of door knocking I had not yet perfected my opening routine. I introduced myself and said I was running for the legislature, but I did not yet realize I needed to add that "I'm here to ask for your vote." Sonja Berg, a member of the St. Cloud City Council, helped straighten me out on this point. So did a few encounters of the following kind.

I was at the door of a man in his thirties in a newly built subdivision in St. Joseph. He looked and sounded like an intelligent and educated person. I said I was running for the legislature in District 14A, handed him the brochure, and went through the rest of the routine. When I finished he said, "What is it you want?" I replied by describing the kind of legislation I hoped to author. He interrupted me and said, "Why are you here?" Only then did I realize that he literally did not understand why I was there. My telling him I was running for the legislature did not register anything that explained what I was doing at his door. From then on I remembered to "ask for your vote," though this person was probably not a voter.

I had a few people tell me straight out they had no idea what the Minnesota Legislature does, and I suspect there were hundreds more who kept their ignorance on this point to themselves. Some individuals' understanding of what I was doing did not go past a vague recognition that it had something to do with "the government," without grasping that there were different levels of government with distinct responsibilities. I had to explain to one man that though it was unfortunate the grass was so high in the city park adjoining his property, this was a matter to take up with his city council, and to another that he would have to talk to someone else about getting cable access. (Several legislators told me that if I won the election, I should expect to be awakened at 4 a.m. by someone telling me the snowplow just knocked over their mailbox.)

As a matter of pure campaign strategy, I should have ended my encounters with the politically clueless as quickly as possible, because they are overwhelmingly nonvoters. But the ingrained habits of a teacher often led me, for better or worse, to stay longer and dispel at least a few fragments of misinformation. One young blue-collar worker was railing against immigration. (Even though the Minnesota Legislature does not set immigration policy, I did not consider national issues of this kind out of bounds for conversation.) After repeating the widely held though false view that immigrants pay no taxes, he continued, "I don't understand why they let all those Haitians into the country when there are white people here who need jobs." Where do you begin? I let the anti-immigrant sentiment alone and instead reminded him that not all native-born Americans were white—which he quickly admitted once I brought it to his attention. I would like to believe I got the message across, whether or not I got his vote (if indeed he voted at all).

There were, however, pathological cases where there was no point in continuing the discussion. One older man, very strange and perhaps unhinged, started to complain about all the stoplights along Division Street in St. Cloud. This stretch of highway is in fact a great irritation, very time consuming to traverse, and as sympathetically as possible I began to explain who had jurisdiction over this matter. He looked at me fiercely and cried, "It's the Jews that did it! The Jews!"

Time to move along to the next door.

Not all ignorance was pathological, however, and at least some of it was pardonable. I did not expect the typical voter to understand immediately the difference between the national health care reforms proposed by Bill Clinton in his campaign for president and Minnesota's recently passed HealthRight program (now MinnesotaCare) to provide subsidized insurance to the working poor. I welcomed conversation about health care reform at either state or national levels. The same applied when someone began talking about the federal budget deficit, which I could easily enough shift to a discussion of the projected state deficit. I did not consider it out of bounds for someone to ask for my opinion of George Bush, Bill Clinton, or Ross Perot. How I answered a question about the presidential candidates might help some voters understand who I was, how I thought about the world, and what kind of legislator I would be, even though my responsibilities if elected were very different from those of national elected officials.

I suspect that many of my efforts as an itinerant, uninvited, and unpaid civics teacher fell on deaf ears. But not all of them. One woman in her twenties, who at first admitted to knowing and caring little about politics, asked me at the end of our conversation how she could subscribe to the Minnesota Legislature's weekly newsletter.

Learning from the Informed

At the opposite extreme from the politician haters and the clueless were the individuals who were well-informed, thoughtful, and eager to talk. I stayed and heard them out, whether or not I agreed with their views, because they helped me clarify my own stance on issues, and because I wanted a reputation as someone who genuinely listened. Some individuals provided valuable general perspective on some broad theme (education, budgets, health care); others supplied me with life stories or local perspective that grafted flesh to my own skeletal understanding of a problem.

Door knocking in Avon in early July, I happened upon the home of the principal of Avon Elementary School. (Had I scheduled an official appointment at his office, he might have been less revealing than he was conversing in his driveway.) He said the first responsibility of the legislature was to determine priorities, and unfortunately education was a slipping priority in Minnesota. So far he had been able to keep class sizes down, but it was a struggle. He then proceeded to the issue of gambling. (Both charitable gambling and Indian casino gambling had tremendously expanded in recent years, and legislators were under pressure to "even the playing field" by legalizing private, for-profit, off-reservation gambling.) He made the following prediction: the Minnesota Legislature, after enacting policies that worsened gambling addiction in the state, would then impose an unfunded mandate on public schools to teach children how to resist the very gambling addiction the legislature had helped worsen. He also talked about the sex education controversy in the Avon-Albany school district: because of irreconcilable differences between advocates of standard and abstinence-only sex education, the school district had to create and fund two separate sex education curricula. He invited me to attend PTA meetings in the fall.

I stopped by his house again in late October. He remembered every detail of our previous conversation and added: "Remember my prediction about gambling education." He said he would vote for me. I do not believe he was a predictable Democratic vote; if anything, he seemed an independent with conservative leanings. It was our personal conversation that won him over.

I was always receptive to anyone who could provide some responsible perspective on how to address the state's budget problems. Predictably, many comments on the budget were simplistic ("just stop spending!") or irresponsible: individuals would simultaneously demand lower taxes, more spending on programs that helped them personally, and cuts to programs that assisted anyone else. I began challenging people who demanded that we "cut spending" to name some program that *they* benefited from that they were willing to cut. Several individuals replied, without irony, that they had never benefited in their life from government spending of any kind.

But I also met many individuals with a well-developed budgetary conscience. A recently retired police chief in St. Joseph, who was equally worried about the national and state deficits, insisted that he "doesn't want any money spent on him" — meaning I should spend state money only on people who really need it. I had several individuals tell me (in persuasive detail) that there was no way to fund adequately the state's transportation network without some increase in the gasoline tax. (This was fifteen years before the I-35 bridge collapse in Minneapolis.)

A large chunk of state revenues went back to cities and counties in the form of local government aid, and it was generally admitted that the state's formula for allocating local government aid penalized thrift and rewarded extravagance. A more rational system of allocating these funds would save the state a significant amount of money, and I listened carefully to anyone who had useful suggestions on this score. A member of the Avon City Council, speaking to me as he watered his garden, told me the state could eliminate a lot of waste by budgeting local government aid before—not after—local units drew up their own budgets, so local officials knew where they stood. An information systems analyst currently teaching at Metropolitan State University (a disillusioned former Democrat who wanted to know if I was "fiscally conservative") believed that wasteful local government expenditures could be remedied by having the state mandate, but also fund, a common computerized system of cost accounting. More anecdotally, mayors and city council members in more than one town told me, "If you want to see how cities get rewarded for wasteful spending, take a look at ——" (out of fondness for the town I withhold the name).

I had an unexpectedly large number of doorstep conversations on the theme of reforming the state's workers' compensation system, and in general about workplace health and safety. Reforming what was perceived to be an overly expensive and confrontational workers' comp system was especially important to owners of small businesses, the largest source of employment in the district. My strong labor support presumptively put me in tension with business owners on this issue. But I went out of my way to signal a willingness to listen to all sides and look for mutually acceptable reforms.

Some business owners revealed more about themselves than anything else. I recorded that one owner of a construction company "railed about workmen's comp fraud—was convinced that workers these days were mostly scoundrels, and he looks forward to getting out of business and not having to deal with them anymore." But more often the advice was offered in a constructive spirit. A contractor I met in Sartell (whom I recorded as a positive contact but added "probably Republican") thought it was possible to reduce workers' compensation costs without cutting benefits by shortening the litigation process and putting more emphasis on retraining injured workers; he recommended that I look into Wisconsin's system. The owner of a sawmill believed the system could be improved by more emphasis on prevention: the regulators "tell us to improve safety but give us no guidance on how to do it."

The issue that generated the most discussion at the doors was health care. Abortion was mentioned slightly more often by voters at the door than health care (see chapter 5). But people who brought up health care wanted to engage me in genuine conversation about the problem. This was less often the case when a voter mentioned abortion.

I received copious quantities of general advice—from doctors, nurses, dentists, hospital administrators, chiropractors, insurance agents, to name a few—about what was wrong with the system and how to fix it. I listened to dozens of health care professionals tell me they supported the goals of HealthRight but opposed funding it by taxing providers. I had a long and civil conversation with an employee of a pharmaceutical company (whom I marked as "definitely Republican," and who I am certain did not vote for me) who insisted that high drug prices simply reflected the costs of research and development and the lack of adequate patent protection. I heard any number of arguments for and against the single-payer proposal or the Canadian model.

But what made a deeper impression were the life stories that left any policy conclusions up to me. In Brockway Township my wife, Pia, and I spoke with a farmer on crutches in a leg cast, the result of a farm accident. He was uninsured at the time of the accident, because the cost was prohibitive, and was still uninsured at the time of our conversation. Affordable health insurance was his chief issue. (He was not a one-issue man, however: he told us he did not like the Minnesota Education Association and complained that the new Sartell high school was designed too much around extracurricular sports.)

I spoke to a couple with a four-year-old girl. The husband was a carpenter, and the wife worked for an optical firm. She did not like her job and would have preferred to stay home with the child, but her job included health care benefits, and his did not. So they were locked into an employment and family arrangement they would not have chosen. This was a very typical case.

In Albany I met a woman who lived with her eighty-year-old mother. The nearby clinic where her mother received regular care was relocating to a hospital much farther away. Did any programs exist, she asked me, for transporting the elderly to hospitals for nonemergency visits? Some kind of "clinic taxi" service?

In Brockway Township I heard a strange and complicated story from a couple who had both worked for a major national retailer before they married. The company told them: "When you get married, one of you must resign," which the couple claimed was marital discrimination. They both resigned and were suing the company. Both had serious medical problems (I wrote down "horrendous story" but didn't record the details), which may have played a role in the company's decision to push them out. They were both looking for work and claimed that the welfare office was "not serious about getting people into jobs. They say, don't take any job unless there's medical benefits involved."

In a similar vein I talked with a man who told me that "welfare should be workfare," and who went on to explain that his brother was manic depressive and could function only if he had psychiatric care. But if his brother worked more than four hours a day, he lost his health benefits, so it did not pay to work.

Perhaps the strangest and most heartbreaking story I heard during six months of door knocking involved discrimination against a child with a correctible disability. A couple in Sartell had a daughter who required special eyeglasses for which contact lenses could not substitute. The child had enrolled in a private dance school and successfully completed the course. But she was told she could not wear eyeglasses at the final public performance because it disrupted the ballet's aesthetics. Because she could not function without glasses, she was barred from the performance. The child was devastated, and her parents outraged.

I visited the couple the first time in June, in the middle of this controversy. I promised I would help in any way I could, whether I won the election or not. I gave them the name and number of someone I knew on the St. Cloud Area Human Rights Commission and said that if this kind of discrimination was not already against the law, it should be. I followed up with a letter, which they remembered and appreciated when I visited them again late in the campaign.

In this case whether solving the problem was ordinarily a state legislator's responsibility was beside the point. (This was not like cable access or uncut grass in a city park.) I believed that when someone was the victim of a clear injustice, their elected representatives — at whatever level of government — had a duty to step in. Even as a mere candidate I felt an obligation to help because they had trusted me enough to tell the story. I recognized that if I were elected, cases like this would add time-consuming responsibilities to my ordinary legislative duties, but I was willing to accept this charge.

A Tense Encounter

When I was a teenager, my grandmother suffered a debilitating stroke and spent the last several years of her life in a succession of depressing and understaffed nursing homes. I do not believe our family had any alternative. But twenty years later, when I was running for office in a district with a large and growing elderly population, my family history predisposed me to consider seriously alternatives to nursing homes.

Budgetary considerations also recommended it: a huge percentage of the state's Medical Assistance budget paid for seniors in nursing homes who had exhausted all family assets. Becky Hooper, one of my campaign volunteers, had worked with a pilot project called Seniors Agenda for Independent Living (SAIL) designed to provide publicly funded in-home care for elderly who were still able to manage without full-time residential care. I endorsed this project in my campaign literature and in mailings targeted to senior-age voters. All of this serves as background to an intriguing pair of encounters I had while door knocking on August 14 in Albany.

A man who appeared to be in his forties or fifties answered the door. He looked over my literature and looked intently at me but was uncommunicative at first. Then without revealing his name, he began quizzing me: what was my position on senior issues? What were my views on nursing homes and alternatives to nursing homes? I proceeded to give an enthusiastic endorsement to the SAIL project. At this point he exploded at me and chewed my head off.

I had walked into a trap. It turns out he was the administrator of Albany's nursing home, and he saw the SAIL project as a financial and ideological attack on his profession. He denied that at-home care was less expensive than residential care, once all at-home costs like food stamps and fuel assistance were taken into account. He wanted the abolition of pre-admissions screening (which determines whether someone really requires nursing home care) because this left nursing homes with only the most expensive and care-intensive patients. "Look, no one *wants* to go into a nursing home," he said. "But sometimes there's no choice, and we have to make it work."

He was also angry that I had not already contacted him to arrange for a tour of the nursing home he managed. (I apologized for the omission and promised to correct it. When later in the campaign he gave me a tour, he seemed genuinely to care about the residents.) The encounter at his door was a long and tense one, and in this case I could not simply cut him off and leave. And oddly enough, despite his rude behavior, I almost felt some sympathy for him given the difficult economics he faced and most people's negative image of nursing homes. He kept pressing me about procedures and regulations of which I clearly knew nothing, and by the end of the encounter he had me half convinced I was an ignoramus on the subject and would have to relearn senior care policy from the beginning.

But the god of poetic justice stepped in. On that same day, a block away on the same street, I called at the home of a man in his seventies who was mostly blind and living alone. He had meals brought in and received some other forms of help. He told me he wanted to keep living at home as long as possible; he definitely did not want to go to a nursing home. A few weeks later in Royalton I met another elderly man, also blind and living alone. He had me read out to him the text of my campaign brochure, then talked to me for a long time about his life. He also did not want to go to a nursing home. I came away convinced my position was the right one, and I stuck with it to the end.

Multi-issue Conversations

My doorstep meetings were not my only source of information on the issues I would face as legislator. I read up on issues whenever I could find the time, and Pia briefed me on her own researches. I interviewed current and former legislators. And I learned as much as I could from representatives of politically organized groups, who were especially eager to share what they knew with first-time candidates. But there are things you can learn from talking with people at their doors that you cannot easily learn any other way.

One thing you get at the door is a glimpse of how someone lives: is it a large new home with a three-car garage, or an old house needing new paint? Are there young children living in the house, or perhaps an elderly parent? Even in a brief visit a candidate forms some impression of an individual voter's life as a whole that cannot be gathered from a phone conversation or the voter's response to a issue survey. And the same effect works in reverse: a voter who speaks with a candidate in person at the door, even briefly, forms an impression (favorable or unfavorable) beyond what could be gathered from a phone conversation, campaign mailing, or radio ad. And of course the fact that the candidate has taken the time to make the call is an important element of the voter's impression.

A good doorstep conversation also reminds you of the political multi-sidedness of individual voters: the range of issues they care about, and how they link one issue to another. A targeted phone survey can record an individual's response to a menu of issues chosen and worded by someone else. But you learn something very different by noting what issues an individual voter brings up, and in what order, when invited into conversation with a candidate at the door.

One August day in Avon Township I spoke with a union plumber whose wife ran a small business. He wanted me to understand that as a union member he saw labor-management issues from one perspective; as co-owner of a small business, he saw them from another; and where they were in tension, as on workers' comp, he was looking for some workable compromise. We also spoke about the abortion issue (it was always the voter, never me, who brought up that theme). I marked down that he "wanted to talk about every category in my flier."

I called on the home of a man who taught industrial arts at a public high school. Our conversation naturally began with education issues: the school system's decision to spend millions on a new football field and a pittance on computer technology for educational use; the disappearance of a work ethic among high school students; the lack of attention to special needs students, both handicapped and gifted. But then he noticed the environment section of my campaign literature and told me he owned property in Crane Meadows, a large unspoiled wetland in Morrison County being considered for national wildlife refuge status. He was ambivalent about the designation, being very attached to the family property there, but said, "If they genuinely manage it as a wildlife refuge, we're for it." He did not want it turned into a hunters' playground. Then he asked me if I would like him to show me his land in Crane Meadows. I agreed, partly to acquaint myself with the wildlife refuge question and partly because it was a chance to campaign in an otherwise out-of-the-way corner of the district. So a few weekends later he graciously showed Pia and me the land and introduced us to some neighboring landowners, some of whom made clear they did not support either the wildlife refuge or me.

I had another multi-issue discussion with a couple who had children in parochial schools and told me they favored vouchers. They owned a small optical firm, and we discussed workers' comp and the difficulties small businesses face getting loans and paying for employee health insurance. They brought up the problem of drunk driving and urged me to support tougher laws. The wife was a licensed day-care provider, and we discussed some regulatory issues. They were probably Republicans. I do not know if they voted for or against me. But I do not believe the election would have been so close unless at least some of these multi-issue conversations had won over people who would not have supported me on one issue alone.

I met a couple who were both schoolteachers. He was in the public system, she at a Catholic school, which gave them an unusual perspective on public versus private education. I spoke with a mortgage lender who was also an elected member of his city council; the two roles mutually reinforced his conviction that groundwater contamination was a serious problem.

These individuals (and couples) were all very different from one another. There is no "typical voter." What they had in common was that they showed me many different sides of their political character—doing so by choice and on their own terms—and in the process brought out many sides of myself as candidate.

For every individual I have profiled and every issue that person mentioned, there exists at least one professional association and/or political action committee that claims to represent their interests and views: teachers' union, plumbers' union, small business association, mortgage lenders' association, an association for local elected officials, not to mention countless organizations that lobby legislatures about drunk driving, protecting wetlands, support for parochial schools, and so on. Professional associations and politically organized action groups play an essential role in our democracy. They study issues and communicate their positions with greater depth and precision than most voters could ever do in a doorstep conversation with a candidate.

But group representation cannot substitute for individual conversations between candidate and voter. A healthy democracy needs both collective action and individual conversation, and it is the latter that is ever in danger of being squeezed out. A professional association or political action committee can only communicate to elected officials *one* side of the individuals they represent. But what professional association represents the interests of schoolteachers who care about protecting wetlands? Or the interests of labor-management married couples? Or mortgage lenders serving on city councils and concerned about groundwater? Legislators—unlike most of the organized groups lobbying them—have to concern themselves with the full range of issues and their interconnections. Most voters also care about many issues and attempt to interconnect them. A healthy democracy needs some venue by which the full-range thinking of voters and the full-range thinking of candidates and representatives can meet and respond to one another.

Facing the Farmers

Door-knocking farms posed special challenges. In a town it typically took only thirty seconds to get from one door to another. Getting from one farmer to the next could sometimes take ten minutes or more. At the end of a long and vehicle-challenging road, I often found no one in the house and had to track down the farmer in the milk barn or out on a tractor. There were frequently delicate negotiations with dogs. When I did locate the farmer, our conversation was often overwhelmed by the noise of machinery. And farmers, more than any other demographic group, made me most conscious of my status as an outsider.

In St. Wendel Township one July afternoon, Pia and I drove down one especially long dirt road to find a farmer sitting in front of the house with a shotgun across his lap. Noting the expression on my face, he explained, "It's for woodchucks." We had a brief conversation in which he revealed very little. He got out of me that I was not born in the area.

My difficulties connecting with farmers were increased by my own inability to engage in small talk about farm operations. I had learned as much about farm *policy* as I could in a short period of time—about how the federal milk pricing system disadvantaged dairy farmers in the upper Midwest, for instance. But about day-to-day farm *operations* I was embarrassingly ignorant. For example, I did not know the difference between—well, I will just leave it at that.

Most of the policy directly affecting farmers was set by the federal government. I typically asked farmers what I could do to help them if I were elected. But the Minnesota Legislature could only assist farmers in marginal ways; they knew it, and I knew it, which narrowed the range of possible conversation. When I did have substantive political conversations with farmers, it was more often about affordable health insurance, which many of them lacked and which I might be able to address as a legislator. At many farms one family member, often the wife, worked a full-time off-farm job to provide health benefits for the rest of the family.

The following conversation with a Holding Township dairy farmer was typical. He spoke at length and in detail about health care costs. They had had to pay $7,000 out of pocket for his wife's cesarean section, including $5 per tablet for aspirin they gave her in the hospital. When we got to milk prices, however, he simply shook his head and said he did not think any one politician could accomplish much.

Of course, some farmers were doing much better than others: some families were slowly being squeezed out, and others were buying up or leasing the land to expand their operation. In Krain Township we met with a father (about sixty) and son (about thirty) at a dairy farm who told us they had never signed on to any federal farm program and had no sympathy whatsoever for farmers who could not make it on their own. We heard a very different story a few farms down the road. In reply to my question about how the Minnesota Legislature could help farmers, a farmer in her forties believed something might be done about the obstacles faced by young farmers just getting started after inheriting a debt-ridden farm. I mentioned by name the father and son I had just spoken with. "They were lucky enough to inherit that farm debt-free," she said. "Most farmers don't."

Many family farms survived only by compromising part of their cherished independence. Farmers who once produced and sold their own milk or beef had shifted in many cases to keeping turkeys on contract for large meat-processing corporations. Where the milk barn once stood, there was now a turkey shed, the change in aroma evident from a half mile away. I did not follow farmers into the turkey shed.

As the number of family farms gradually decreased, the land was often sold and subdivided for residential developments. This led to predictable conflicts. A farmer who was on the board of St. Wendel Township (the scene of exploding residential sprawl) described how people would build new houses in the middle of farm areas, then complain about the smell of manure as though the farmers had just moved in.

Farmers would occasionally surprise me by raising some issue I could never have imagined. One August day in Brockway Township I had two different farmers tell me I should pass a law automatically granting every farmer a free deer-hunting license. "We feed them. We should be allowed to shoot them." I said I would think about it.

Enforcing the Election Code

Contacting apartment dwellers presented challenges of a very different kind. If farmers were the most rooted group of prospective voters, apartment dwellers were the most rootless. The turnover rate in any apartment complex was high: someone you talked with in August may very well have moved out of district by November. And even those who stayed were on average less connected with the community and less likely to vote than homeowners. For this reason many legislative candidates skipped apartments altogether or relegated them to group door-knocks or literature drops.

But I did my best to include apartment buildings in my door-knocking plans. There were potentially a lot of votes there. In a good-size apartment complex you could make fifty contacts in an hour, which helped offset the higher percentage of nonvoters and transients. And simply on principle, I believed apartment dwellers deserved representation as much as anyone else did. We ourselves lived in an apartment at the time. These were so to speak "my people"; if they were transients, so was I.

The real problems came not from apartment dwellers but from apartment building managers. Nearly every apartment building has a "no soliciting" policy. Managers of apartment buildings and the rental companies that employ them see no difference between a candidate for office door-knocking for votes and a door-to-door salesman hawking vacuum cleaners. They interpret the "no soliciting" policy as equally forbidding both and routinely do everything they can to prevent candidates from campaigning in their apartment buildings.

This is in fact against the law. Minnesota's Fair Campaign Practices code (section 211B.20, Denial of Access by Political Candidates to Multiple Unit Dwellings) specifically entitles candidates who have filed for public office to go door-to-door in apartment buildings and college dormitories to communicate with prospective voters. The law permits residential managers to request appointments and restrict campaigning to reasonable hours but does not permit them categorically to forbid access to the entire apartment or dormitory complex. The law grants access rights only to the candidate in person, not to volunteers campaigning in the candidate's absence. Any individual apartment dweller may of course refuse to speak with a candidate. The rationale behind the law is that to deny candidate access to multi-unit dwellings is to deprive apartment dwellers of effective representation. It is not merely a matter of a candidate's right to solicit votes but also of a *voter's* right to be informed and to hold elected officials accountable. If an apartment manager denies access to candidates—or even worse, allows access to favored candidates and denies others—this right is violated.

The law is a good one. Unfortunately apartment managers routinely violate it and in many cases do not know the law exists, which is the fault of the rental company that employs them. Universities — my own included, until we convinced them to change the policy — sometimes skirt the law by prohibiting candidates from door knocking in dormitories and instead restricting them to dining halls and football games, as though the university's responsibility was to "protect" voting-age students from the dirty business of politics instead of encouraging them to participate in it.

Because of general unwillingness to honor the law, I would simply ignore the "no soliciting" sign and enter apartment buildings when I could, or have someone who lived there let me in. But I had several confrontations with apartment managers. The manager of a large, multi-building apartment complex in Sartell told me to leave or he would have me arrested for trespassing. I explained the law to him. He said he had never heard of it, and I am sure he believed I was making this up. I continued to insist that *he* was violating the law, and if he persisted, *I* would contact the police — as though the Sartell police department would dispatch squad cars with sirens blaring to punish violations of the election code. We calmed down, exchanged names and addresses, and I followed up with a letter that included the actual text of the law and public authorities he could contact if he doubted me. In accordance with the law's provisions I requested an appointment. To his credit, he admitted his mistake and later allowed me to campaign in the apartment complex.

Running Short of Time

Door knocking was the one reliable constant in a long campaign in which everything else was unpredictable. But the pace and tone of my doorstep discourse changed over time. When I began door knocking in late April, I was still the only declared candidate for an open seat. When people asked me, "Who are you running against?" I could not answer their question. I was a complete unknown, and my reputation in the district, for better or worse, depended on me alone. By midsummer I had an opponent, but to most voters the election still seemed far away; some had to be reminded this was an election year. Conversations were unhurried in the lazy summer afternoons. People gave me ice water and home-grown strawberries and showed me their flower gardens. It was light until nine at night. I believed I had all the time in the world.

By mid-October of a presidential election year most people were already saturated with campaign rhetoric, and I had to compete with Bush and Clinton and Perot for a few crumbs of attention. I was now in a heated race. The very effectiveness of my door knocking had aroused the opposition. At an event in St. Paul around Labor Day I was introduced to Steve Sviggum, the minority leader (Republican) of the Minnesota House. He said he had "heard good things about me." This was in one sense a genuine tribute across party lines to hard work and effective campaigning. But I suspect it also meant that Republicans in the district were calling him up and saying, "Read's been to my door twice! Where's our guy?"

By late September the opposition had matched or exceeded our campaign with mail, phone calls, and yard signs — though never with door knocking. Literature drops, mass mailings, and phone campaigns by independent political groups supporting my opponent and attacking me (especially on abortion and gun issues) began to rival in quantity and expenditure what either campaign was putting out in its own name. I was no longer fully in control of my own reputation. Political deliberation with voters had to compete with damage control.

Every minute of the day was scheduled (Pia and I were both back teaching full-time), and urgent tasks were neglected for lack of time. I chose not to door-knock in the dark (lest I be considered a weirdo), so the prime daytime hours had to be booked as tightly as possible; after the sun set, I contacted voters by phone, which lacked the warmth and openness of visits in person. My contacts were briefer and more task-oriented: my notes from September and October record fewer substantive conversations and focus instead on who had and had not committed to vote for me. We did group door-knocks of whole towns (by a dozen volunteers wearing Jim Read for State Representative T-shirts). These were fun and created an impression of momentum. But they worked best if they reinforced an earlier visit from me in person, and the hourglass on that was quickly running out.

The activity that to my greatest regret was squeezed out by the time demands after Labor Day was the handwritten letters I sent to individuals with whom I had had substantive conversations. If I could have somehow bought one more hour every day in September and October, that is how I would have used the time.

These letters varied in length and topic, but there were several constants. They had to be addressed by name to the person with whom I had spoken, and had to be sent within a day or two of the visit. They had to be handwritten. They had to refer to several items we had actually talked about. Voters are used to being inundated with "personalized" political mailings that address them by name but are simply canned letters with the same tired rhetoric. A genuinely personal letter is all the more effective because it exposes the falseness of all the others.

I would select perhaps four or five conversations from a day's door knocking for follow-up letters. Writing the letters, verifying the names and addresses, hand-addressing, and mailing them would take about an hour. In the summer I had that hour, and in the fall I no longer did. (I would quote from these letters, but I neglected to keep copies.)

Only occasionally did I get a reply, though people definitely remembered the letters and mentioned them when I made a return visit. One young woman, though, with whom I had spoken in Holdingford and to whom I had sent a handwritten follow-up, replied with a wonderful letter of her own that began:

> Dear Jim, I really appreciate you taking time out of your busy schedule to write me a very nice letter. I was very surprised and enthused how you take interest in people and their views. One thing to always keep in mind is to push for the lower and middle class people, since there are many more of us than the upper class and that means more votes now and in the future. . . . I'm very optimistic that I will be addressing you as our State Representative after the election.

I especially like the detail here about her being "surprised and enthused" that a candidate for office would actually take an interest in people and their views. That is certainly what I always tried to do, and I am pleased that at least sometimes the message got across.

No Electronic Substitute

I have tried to describe here the texture of my personal conversations with thousands of voters over the course of a six-month door-knocking campaign. I believed then, and still believe today, that such conversations are essential to a healthy democracy. They need not and cannot occur in the same way in campaigns for every level of elected office. But they need to occur sometime, somewhere, in our democratic system.

And wherever possible they should occur in person. Much has been written, both insightful and foolish, about the revolutionary potential of the Internet for politics. Clearly in some respects these new technologies have transformed the political landscape. But in the most important respect nothing has changed.

In 1992 the Internet was still in its infancy as a political tool. The blogosphere did not yet exist. Most of the voters I met in 1992 were not computer literate, and few had access to e-mail. My own campaign literature listed my mailing address and home phone number but no Web site. Today nearly every legislative campaign has a Web site with a candidate biography and position statements, and many feature blogs of the campaign. If I were running today, I would use all of these new technologies.

These new technologies can supplement door knocking but cannot replace it. The same goes for TV and radio ads, targeted mailings, billboards, literature drops, phone surveys, mass e-mails, and so on. The undecided voters I most needed to reach would not be persuaded to vote for me unless I showed up in person at their door. A Web site is an effective tool for coordinating the efforts of already committed activists. Political blogs allow for the rapid communication of information among political insiders. But the voters I needed to persuade would not have frequented Web sites like "Minnesota DFLers Blog" or "Minnesota Democrats Exposed" or "Pawlenty Unplugged" even if their equivalents had existed in 1992. The blogosphere is ideologically polarized: activists mutually reinforce already shared views while flaming the opponent from a safe distance.

With door knocking it is precisely the opposite. You are forced every day to meet human beings whose political views differ from your own. At every door you may have to answer a critic or rethink your views. There is no retreat to a comfort zone where you hear only the opinions of supporters and partisans.

I do not want to overly idealize the personal politics of a door-knocking campaign. Many of the conversations were trivial or simpleminded. Many voters are not interested in political deliberation. And some legislative candidates in their door knocking do not actively seek to engage voters in dialogue to the extent I did but simply want to establish name and face recognition. (And of course this was one of my goals too.)

I should also acknowledge that personal politics has its dark side, its own peculiar potential for abuse (as we will discover near the end of this narrative). If personal encounters between candidates and voters create a space for democratic deliberation, they also harbor the potential for mischief, intimidation, and slander. You can explore ideas in a doorstep conversation that the print and electronic media will never communicate. You can also tell lies that the media is not in the position to correct. Every good thing can be abused, and the politics of personal contact is no exception.

Nothing guarantees that genuine communication and deliberation will take place when as a candidate for public office you call upon voters at their door. All you provide is the opportunity. The opportunity may be accepted, declined, or postponed to some indefinite future occasion. Most importantly you are extending the opportunity to *every* eligible voter you hope to represent. Somewhere in our grand democratic edifice there should be a niche reserved for this.

CHAPTER THREE

Media Messages

In mid-October we began running the following thirty-second radio ad, which we titled "New Shoes." I wrote the script and played myself in the ad. Pia was Voice One, the narrator, and Voice Two was Charlotte Fisher, a campaign volunteer, nurse, and health care activist.

VOICE ONE: In the last six months Jim Read, candidate for state representative, has visited almost seven thousand homes. *(door-knock sound)*

JIM READ: Hello, my name is Jim Read. I visited you in June, and I'm here again to ask for your vote.

VOICE TWO: Yes, I remember we talked about health care. You're working pretty hard, aren't you?

JIM READ: Hardworking people deserve a hardworking representative.

VOICE TWO: Well, you've got my vote. And Jim?

JIM READ: Yes?

VOICE TWO: You're going to need some new shoes.

VOICE ONE: Vote for Jim Read on November 3. Paid for by Jim Read Campaign Committee.

Many voters I subsequently contacted at their doors told me they had heard this ad and liked it. "Hardworking people deserve a hardworking representative" was my campaign slogan, and the purpose of the ad was to remind people that I was indeed working hard. The dialogue was corny but effective because it was true: a large proportion of voters who heard the ad had actually talked with me at their doors, many of them more than once. The part about needing new shoes was also true.

Media in a Low-Profile Race

The role of media in a door-knocking campaign like mine was altogether different than in high-profile campaigns for national or statewide office. The continuous mass media attention we are used to in presidential campaigns and hotly contested statewide races was completely absent in my race. There was no television coverage and were no television ads.[1] Large-circulation daily newspapers paid only sporadic attention: the *St. Cloud Times,* for example, mentioned my race in news stories only about once a month, usually very briefly. In high-profile races, mass media coverage has become increasingly obsessed with opinion polls (typically at the expense of issue analysis). In my race polling data were never mentioned in any news story because no public polls were ever taken. The campaigns did their own internal polling and kept the results to themselves.

For a state legislative candidate there are both advantages and disadvantages to this nearly complete exclusion from mass media coverage. The obvious disadvantage is that media silence reinforces the already scant attention many voters pay to state legislative races. The offsetting advantage is that as a candidate running a door-knocking campaign in a low-profile race, you have much more freedom to craft and deliver your own message without the distorting effects of sound-bite journalism. In the competition for limited voter attention span, your advantage is the in-person visit: one or two good conversations between a voter and a living, breathing candidate at the door might equal ten television ads promoting a high-profile candidate the voter never meets.

I do not mean that media played no role in a campaign like mine. In a door-knocking–focused campaign, media skillfully employed fulfills the essential but subordinate function of reinforcing the in-person meetings with voters. My "New Shoes" radio ad, for instance, would have made little impression by itself, but it made a deeper impact by reinforcing an actual visit. Voters who have met you have to be reminded that they have met you and need to be able to distinguish your name from your opponent and a dozen names of candidates in other races.

Some forms of media are fully in the candidate's control, others less so. The first category would include campaign literature handed out at the door, mailings, print and radio ads, yard signs, stickers, T-shirts, and so on. The second category would include newspaper and radio coverage, appearances on radio call-in shows, parades, the letters page of a newspaper, and public candidate forums. Campaign or party-sponsored phone surveys, which are essential in generating good lists of supporters, opponents, and undecideds, could also be classified as "media" because they involve mediated communications between campaigns and voters, in contrast to immediate, in-person conversations between voter and candidate.

Defining Myself

All forms of campaign media need to advance the central goal of defining *who you are* and how you differ from the opponent. The most difficult and essential task, especially if you are running for the first time, is to create yourself as a candidate: to explain convincingly, both to voters and to yourself, why you are running and why you should be the one to represent the people who inhabit this particular patch of territory. You must be able to do this concisely, both in writing (a sentence or two) and orally (in ten seconds or less).

Defining oneself is a task faced by all candidates for public office, from city council all the way up to president. But self-definition in a race like mine was subject to different constraints than in other types of campaigns. First of all, a majority of the electorate would be meeting me in person and judging for themselves whether the self-presentation in my campaign literature fit the person they were meeting at the door.

Second, as a rookie candidate for public office, I was facing this task of public self-creation for the first time.[2] No matter how well-versed one is on political issues as a private citizen — even a private citizen who teaches politics for a living — there is an enormous gulf between engaging with those issues as an individual and facing them as a candidate. In running for office I wanted to remain true to myself. But the new "self" you grow as a candidate is not exactly the same as your old, private self, and it takes some time to discover how to be true to this second, acquired self. For this reason my initial attempts to define myself as a candidate were awkward and painful.

Finally, my position as a newcomer and outsider to the community made the task of explaining who I was and why I was running especially crucial. The easiest, if also least imaginative, answer to "who are you and why are you running?" is something like this: I embody this community and its values. My opponent's campaign perfectly exemplified this approach. His campaign slogan was "Elect Steve Dehler—He's one of us!" (in contrast to you-know-who). "As someone who has spent my entire life in Stearns County," his campaign literature went on to say, "your concerns are my concerns, and your goals for our communities the same as mine." One can of course debate whether long-term residence in a community is the same as understanding its interests and needs, and whether everyone living in a community has the same goals. But whatever the merits of this slogan, that route was closed off to me from the outset. I would have been laughed out of town if I had tried to pass myself off as a deeply rooted member of the Stearns County community. I had to define very differently who I was and why I should be selected to represent a community into which I had been so recently transplanted.

Defining myself as a candidate was a process of trial and error with some embarrassing false starts. My first literature piece was produced for the local party conventions in April, when we still assumed the incumbent, Bernie Omann, would be the opponent. It was heavy on issues: there were headings for health, education, environment, agriculture, labor, small business, and seniors, with much policy-wonkish detail under each heading. But my unifying theme was pretty lame. Because Omann was an incumbent, my opening line was, "Politics is too important to be left to the incumbents." I have never been an incumbent basher; this slogan now seems to me a transparent attempt to exploit the anti-incumbent mood of the time. Because his legislative salary was his principal source of income (whereas if elected I would continue to teach half the year), I characterized Omann as a "professional politician." As a final irrefutable reason to vote for me rather than Omann, the best I could do was, "We Can Do Better!" Omann's decision to run for Congress allowed me to erase this uninspiring first attempt and start over.

My next attempt at a unifying campaign theme was "respecting our traditions and looking to our future." In a print ad I placed in the *Morrison*

County Record in July I emphasized that "I grew up in a small town" (I didn't mention the town was in Indiana) and that as a legislator I would combine respect for tradition with a "spirit of innovation." The part about "small town" and "respect for tradition" comes off as defensive, more an attempt at damage control than an affirmative reason to vote for me.

I was also defensive at first about my educational record and professional accomplishments. At the beginning of the campaign there were spirited debates among my campaign volunteers about whether I should list my Harvard Ph.D. on my campaign literature, and whether I should describe myself as a "college professor" or merely as a "teacher." Some of my campaign volunteers argued that in rural Stearns County, where most voters did not have a college degree, intellectuals were held in suspicion and that listing my Harvard Ph.D. would mean electoral death. I had experienced this suspicion myself. One old-time dairy farmer and former Democratic legislative candidate had verbally thrashed me over the phone when he discovered I was a teacher. "You've probably never dug a ditch in your life!" he exclaimed, which was true.

But some other volunteers argued that I had to put the Harvard Ph.D. on the campaign literature. For one thing, there was little else I could point to besides my work as local party chair—none of the ordinary community activities and memberships. More importantly, one campaign volunteer argued, "It's an accomplishment. People respect accomplishments. And this distinguishes you from your opponent" (Dehler lacked a college degree). So in the end I listed the Harvard Ph.D. but did not trumpet it, and described myself as a "college teacher"—that term sounding less pretentious than "professor."

The idea for my final and most successful campaign theme, the one I inserted into the "New Shoes" script, came to us only gradually. We could not have imagined this theme at the beginning, because it grew out of our lived experience of the campaign over time. The theme was, "Hardworking People Deserve a Hardworking Representative." This went on the campaign brochure I was distributing by late summer and stayed in all my ads and literature pieces for the remainder of the campaign.

For example, the radio ad we began running around Labor Day featured several people, all supporters, saying their names and describing what kind of work they did, and concluding with the "hardworking" slogan in my voice. In the local weeklies we were simultaneously running a Labor Day print ad that began, "On Labor Day I salute the working people of central Minnesota" followed by a list of more than thirty occupations (homemakers, electricians, farmers, secretaries . . .) and closing with "Hardworking People Deserve a Hardworking Representative."

What made this campaign theme work was that it highlighted the enormous amount of door knocking I had done, in contrast to my opponent, who had personally visited far fewer doors. My slogan was indisputably true and authentic, which helped dispel the typical voter's cynicism toward the claims politicians make about themselves. Thousands of voters in the district were in a position to know that I had been to their door once or twice and my opponent not at all. If my opponent's slogan "Vote for Steve Dehler—He's one of us!" communicated a clear if unspoken contrast to me, my slogan "Hardworking People Deserve a Hardworking Representative" likewise communicated a contrast. (By pointing out how hard I was working over the summer, the slogan also helped dispel a common though false assumption that teachers do not work very hard and do not work at all in the summer.)

The "hardworking" theme gave people in the district a reason to vote for me even though I was a newcomer and outsider. It said in effect, "All this time and energy you see me putting into this campaign, I will put to work for you and your community if you elect me." Instead of talking around what made me different from the community, this slogan highlighted what the people of the district and I had in common: most people consider themselves to be hardworking, and they notice and respect it in others. At one door in Holding Township in late summer a man looked at the brochure, noted my slogan, and said, "Well, I'm a hardworking guy myself, so we match up pretty well."

Hitting upon this campaign theme also had a therapeutic effect for Pia and me. We had indeed been working unbelievably hard and often had to fight off exhaustion and resentment at how much of our personal and social lives had been sacrificed to the campaign. By making "hardworking" our campaign theme, we were able to turn exhaustion into pride.

The Literature Piece

A literature piece handed out at the door has to accomplish at least two things. If no one is home, it has to convey name and face and prove the candidate was there ("sorry I missed you" in my handwriting). But the impact of a literature piece without personal contact is minimal. If someone does answer the door, the literature piece needs to facilitate conversation and reinforce name and face recognition after the conversation is over.

The campaign brochure we used from late summer through the election was Pia's brainchild. It folded to four inches by eleven inches with my photo and "Jim Read for State Representative" and "Hardworking People Deserve a Hardworking Representative" on the front face. On the back face was a brief resume and contact information. Opening the first fold revealed an eight-by-eleven-inch face with four issue boxes: Health Care, Jobs and Taxes, Education, and Environment, with as much substance on each as I could fit in a four-by-five-inch space. Opening the second fold revealed an eleven-by-seventeen-inch page whose central feature was a map of the district that named all the cities and townships. Radiating from nine widely dispersed spots on the map were arrows leading to photos of supporters, with name and occupation, who lived in that part of the district. The supporters ranged widely in age and type of work. Beside each photo was a quote from each individual, all of which they wrote themselves, explaining why they were supporting me.

The map of the district was especially useful to me in generating conversation at doors. Because of the recent redistricting, very few people knew the boundaries of the district. I would often start a conversation about the new district lines as an excuse to show them the map, which they could not look at without noticing the photos and endorsements. Above the map was a photo of me walking in a parade. On one side of the photo it said, "I began door-knocking on the first of May and have visited 50 houses every day since then. I invite conversation and try to learn something new from everyone I meet." On the other side of the photo it said, "I go the extra mile to meet and talk with you and I'll work just as hard as your representative." On the space below the map was my explanation of why I was running, which emphasized restoring trust in government: "I believe that all candidates for public office, whatever their party and whatever their views, must conduct themselves in a way that restores faith in our political system. I hope to earn your trust as well as your vote." To the right was a photo of Pia ("You need to show them you're married," one legislator told me), and to the left a photo of us with my parents and the antique Chrysler with which they escorted me in the St. Cloud Wheels, Wings, and Water parade. We received lots of positive commentary on this lit piece, both from political insiders and voters at the door.

Parades and Balloons

Parades play a central part in the collective life of small towns in Minnesota. Large cities also have parades, of course. But they have many other forms of entertainment that small towns lack. Small towns understand that there is something interesting and entertaining simply in a community displaying itself to itself. And they are generous enough to count candidates for office as members of the community.

I marched in at least six parades within or near the district during summer 1992. We arranged the campaign schedule so that I would be in a town during the days leading up to and immediately following that town's parade. This timing worked well. When I shook hands with spectators along the parade route, many would remind me that I had just been at their door, and in the days following the parade many people at the door specifically mentioned seeing me in the parade. Almost no one votes for a candidate simply because they have seen that candidate in a parade. But as a method of reinforcing my door-knocking contacts, parades were very effective.

Two volunteers would march in front carrying my banner. Four or five volunteers would proceed along the sideline distributing 2.5-by-3.5-inch adhesive stickers with my name and a map of the district. (Few spectators knew the district lines or which parading candidate was running for what office, so we considered this an important public service.) I would walk behind, working the crowd, and then run to catch up to my parade slot before I was trampled by the high school band behind me.

Parades were fun, but the balloons were not. I had grown up watching national party conventions on television, and I considered it a law of nature that political campaigns required balloons. And what better place to distribute balloons than a parade? We had major balloon-distribution operations for our first two parades, Sartell and St. Joseph. Unfortunately, the balloons were very time-consuming to inflate, and during the parade the strings would get tangled in the wind and become difficult to separate.

To make things worse, we got ourselves into trouble with the Girl Scouts. Minnesota campaign law prohibits campaigns from giving away anything "of economic value" to voters. We made a judgment call that helium balloons were of negligible economic value and so could be given away. Unfortunately, the Girl Scouts judged otherwise and were attempting raise funds by selling balloons for fifty cents apiece in the Sartell parade. We were ahead of them in the parade, and our giving away free balloons undermined their fund-raising market. I later sent a letter of apology to the Girl Scout leader along with a personal contribution: guilt money.

Many people have asked me, "If you knew then what you know now, what is the one thing you would have done differently in your campaign?" I answer, in all seriousness, "No balloons."

Local Newspapers and Radio

Small-circulation local newspapers (typically published weekly or every other week) were important media of communication for my campaign, but more as vehicles for paid campaign ads and letters to the editor than for news stories. Campaign coverage for weekly newspapers like the *Morrison County Record* and the *Stearns-Morrison Enterprise* consisted of an announcement of candidacy, which simply reprinted the text of the campaign's own press release, then in June a simple list of candidates who had filed with the secretary of state's office, a report of primary results in September, general election results in November. In my race there was also notice of a recount and its results.

To a certain extent, this thin election coverage resulted from lack of staffing. But at least equally important were the paper's own priorities and the attitude of its editor. The extreme case here was the *Cold Spring Record*. (Cold Spring was just outside my district, but the *St. Cloud Times,* the *Morrison County Record,* and several other essential papers and radio stations were also located outside the district.) The policy of the *Cold Spring Record* was to print as news without alteration whatever an incumbent submitted (in this case Jeff or Joe Bertram). But anything a challenger submitted was considered political advertising, and the paper demanded that it be paid for. This policy applied even to letters to the editor written by a supporter of a nonincumbent candidate: the paper charged money to print them. Our campaign avoided the *Cold Spring Record* altogether: we never advertised there, and as far as I know they never acknowledged that our campaign existed. Most other weeklies were fairer in their treatment of nonincumbents but still favored incumbents by printing their press releases as news stories.

At one point in the campaign I called an editor or reporter with the *Morrison County Record* asking for more coverage of the Read-Dehler campaign. (The paper was published out of district in Little Falls, but its circulation area included the lower third of Morrison County, which was in my district.) She told me the paper lacked the staff to cover campaigns. The closest the paper came was to publish candidates' answers to three questions put to them by the newspaper: Did we favor term limits? Did we favor legalizing video gambling off reservation? What would we do to correct the state's budget deficit? (Abortion was conspicuously absent from the list in an area known for antiabortion activism — a quiet act of protest against single-issue politics on the part of the editors.) News coverage in the *Stearns-Morrison Enterprise* (published in-district in Albany) never went beyond the announcement of candidacy and a report of election results.

The lack of genuine news coverage by the small local papers was not a serious problem, because their advertising rates were affordable and with our own ads we could communicate directly with their readers, many of whom scrutinized ads more closely than news stories anyway. This made the small papers more valuable to us in many respects than the *St. Cloud Times,* whose advertising rates were too expensive for us and whose news coverage of my race was spotty.

But lack of resources alone does not explain small papers' lack of campaign coverage. It is in the end a question of priorities. This was proved by the very extensive and careful coverage of the Read-Dehler campaign by the *St. Joseph Newsleader,* which had no more (probably less) staffing resources than the other papers. It helped that both candidates lived in St. Joseph, but other towns presumably had an equal stake in the election's outcome.

The *Newsleader*'s editor at that time, Stuart Goldschen, was like me a recent transplant to the area, without family roots. He edited the newspaper, wrote most of the stories, distributed it, and promoted it (though he was not its owner). Under his editorship the *Newsleader* became something completely different than it had been before he arrived. His approach to news was to pursue in great depth and over a long period of time a few stories that he judged interesting or important. He paid scant attention to many other things that are typically reported in small-town newspapers, which made him unpopular in some quarters.

But from my perspective as a candidate, his coverage was exemplary. He decided the Read-Dehler contest was an important story and reported on it in depth at all stages of the campaign. He interviewed both candidates several times, reporting our words accurately and at length on a wide range of issues, including each candidate's responses to statements made by the other. He included excellent coverage of our October 6 debate, election results, the recount, and the candidates' final reflections. The *Newsleader* articles in my campaign scrapbook are an indispensable source in writing this memoir. If other small-town papers pay far less attention to legislative campaigns, it is because their editors do not consider campaigns as interesting as Goldschen did.

There was only one radio station located within my district, KASM in Albany. The station's morning host, Cliff Mitchell, broadcast a brief phone interview with me when I announced my candidacy. Off-microphone he explained I would be invited to be a guest on his hour-long "Party Line" interview and call-in show sometime in October on the condition that my campaign bought advertising time with the station, which seemed fair enough since we intended to advertise there anyway. Paul Stacke at WJON (St. Cloud) hosted a similar interview and call-in show. Both Mitchell and Stacke were good interviewers and genuinely interested in issues. (My KASM appearance played a fateful role late in the campaign, which I describe in chapter 5.) KLTF in Little Falls hosted an afternoon candidate forum in October, which it broadcast live. Minnesota Public Radio's local station KNSR, located at St. John's campus (just out of district), broadcast some decent-length segments of our October 6 candidate forum. There were dozens of other St. Cloud–area radio stations but, except for the four named above, none paid any attention to the Read-Dehler campaign. We only purchased ad time on three stations: KASM, because it was the only in-district station and reached the farm vote; WJON in St. Cloud, because of its older, more politically engaged listeners; and KLTF in Little Falls, because we needed some ad play in Morrison County.

Both St. John's University and the College of St. Benedict had their own student newspapers at that time: the St. Ben's *Independent* and the St. John's *Record*. Both papers included stories on the campaign during late spring and in the fall (the papers were not published in the summer). The student papers were most useful to us as a location for paid ads. Minnesota allows for election day registration, and students can declare their campus address their residence, but many students do not know this and unless informed otherwise assume that they can only vote in their parents' hometown. We needed a good student turnout, and late in the campaign we placed full-page ads in both student papers explaining the election day registration procedures and listing polling locations.

The *St. Cloud Times* was the region's only daily newspaper, and it had a circulation around thirty thousand. St. Cloud itself was not in district 14A (it was just over the district boundary), but a high percentage of house-holds in the district subscribed to the *Times*. The paper understandably paid more attention to legislative races in St. Cloud, but it recognized that District 14 lay in its circulation area. The paper ran a brief but substantive story on my announcement for office in March, and my opponent's in June. For most of the summer, however, the paper printed very little about state legislative campaigns. My name turned up briefly when I filed for office in June, and again in September in a quick list of how much money area candidates had raised. There was brief coverage of our October 6 debate. There were more stories on the election results and recount than there were in the two months preceding the election.

Each election contest was allocated one feature article during the campaign; the 14A campaign story came on October 13. Unfortunately the reporter was inexperienced, understood little of politics, and was careless in reporting my words. My insistence that I refused to be labeled either "pro-choice" or "pro-life" on the abortion issue somehow turned up in the story as, "Read stresses he is neither for nor against abortion"—a stupid statement I never made and that was subsequently quoted against me in letters to the editor by supporters of my opponent.

Letters to the Editor

The letters page of the newspaper is an especially important forum for local campaigns. The sparse or nonexistent coverage of a legislative campaign in regular news stories raises the relative profile of the letters page; a candidate mentioned once a month in news stories might be endorsed, or criticized, several times a week in the letters page of a daily paper. A letter for or against a presidential candidate usually does not tell readers anything they do not already know. But a letter recommending a legislative candidate submitted by a local writer (known in his or her community) who can speak about the candidate from personal experience conveys new and potentially decisive information to many readers. It is not unusual for someone who has published a letter to the editor on behalf of a local candidate to get follow-up phone calls from other members of the community (calls that can, of course, be either pleasant or hostile). A letter writer stakes his or her name and public reputation; that is the whole point.

Newspapers often will not run a letter from the candidate himself or herself; candidates have to pay for ad space. But most papers will carry letters from supporters as long as they can verify name and address and the letters are not obviously "canned." Most of the time campaign volunteers do their essential work far from the public eye, while the candidate's name is on public display. The letters page reverses this by giving an individualized public voice to supporters. A candidate should never forget that every campaign volunteer has his or her own reasons for supporting a particular candidate and sacrificing time from other activities. The letters page allows supporters to explain publicly why they believe electing this candidate is worth their time and effort.

Unfortunately some campaign managers fail to understand this and instead treat letter writers as mere cogs in the campaign's own wheel. In my years as local party chair I received far too many requests — sometimes from legislative campaigns, sometimes from statewide campaigns — soliciting volunteers to "sign" letters to the editor penned by campaign operatives. (And I suspect that campaigns in rival parties have made similar requests.) It is easy to understand why this happens. An effective letter to the editor is difficult to write, and many people will promise a campaign they will do it and not follow through. Busy campaign managers assume it will speed up the process if they draft the letters themselves and ask supporters for nothing more than the use of their name.

But such letters are far less effective than authentic ones. They sound like a party's or campaign's own press releases and make little impression on a reader. They also encourage laziness and undermine the qualities of active citizenship. Any campaign that talks about "empowering citizens" and then pressures supporters to sign canned letters is undermining its own message. The fact that good letters are time-demanding to write is precisely what makes them effective: they cannot be faked. And any newspaper op-ed page with the staffing resources to read letters and verify them will reject canned letters anyway.

Our campaign actively solicited letters to the editor supporting me; we did not leave this to chance. But we never drafted a letter for anyone simply to sign. Instead, we sent out a list of pointers on writing good letters. Most importantly we stressed that a letter writer should make clear in what context he or she knew or had observed me. For example, Jim Graeve's October 28 letter in the *St. Cloud Times* began by reporting that he had door-knocked with me the past two Saturdays in Albany and Sartell. "Countless times, people from both communities informed me that they had met Read personally when he had been to see them at their home." Carolyn Reeck's October 26 letter compared how both candidates had responded to a question about wetlands she asked at the St. Joseph debate.

Though many newspapers will not publish letters directly from the candidate, papers sometimes allow a candidate to reply to misstatements of fact in letters submitted by someone else. One letter to the *Morrison County Record* by a supporter of my opponent falsely claimed that I had lived in the area for only two years, in contrast to my opponent who had lived there his entire life. I could have responded but let it pass. "This is false. I have in fact lived in central Minnesota for four years!" does not make a crushingly effective reply.

Phoning, Classifying, and Targeting

The media forms described so far—general-purpose campaign brochures, print and radio ads, letters to the editor, parades, and newspaper coverage—are both old-fashioned and broadly directed: every newspaper subscriber, radio listener, and parade spectator receives the same message. Door knocking, of the kind described in chapter 2, is also a broadly targeted campaign technique: the candidate's goal is to meet and speak with as many of the district's eligible voters as possible. In doorstep conversations the campaign's broad message can of course be tailored to the needs and interests of individual voters.

But campaign practice is always changing, and techniques developed for high-profile campaigns filter down to local races. One such technique is the use of phone surveys to classify voters not just into supporters, opponents, and undecideds but also according to where they stand on key issues and how they rank these issues in their voting decisions. Armed with this information, a campaign can then tailor its message to each voter with personalized mailings and persuasion calls specifically addressing that voter's key concerns.

In many respects this technique functions to fill the vacuum created by the long-term decline in ordinary voters' attachment to political parties. In older, stronger political parties, the party's precinct captain was expected to know the individual voters in the precinct and adapt the party's message to their needs, concerns, and prejudices. Today, when local political parties are weak and precinct chairs often nonexistent, parties and campaigns naturally look for other ways to connect with individual voters.

For presidential, statewide, and congressional campaigns, where most voters will never meet the candidate, this technique may be the most efficient way to individualize the campaign message. For a door-knocking–centered state legislative campaign, survey-generated voter profiles can be a valuable supplement to the candidate's own conversations with voters at the door. But given scarce time and money, a legislative campaign armed with precise classification of voters may be tempted to forego door knocking altogether or employ it only in narrowly targeted ways.

This technique was relatively new, at least for the Minnesota DFL Party, when I ran for office in 1992. Specific techniques have evolved over time; the description that follows should not be taken as state-of-the-art campaign practice. And my access to the technique even in its 1992 form was limited and spotty. But the fundamental purpose behind classifying and targeting voters has not changed since 1992.

The purpose of the phone surveys employed by the Minnesota DFL Party was to determine a voter's party affiliation, his or her views on a range of key issues, and "if the election were held today," who he or she would vote for in a number of contests (president, governor, U.S. Senate, U.S. House of Representatives, state legislature—though there were no U.S. Senate or gubernatorial races in Minnesota in 1992). The value of the information depended on its being gathered objectively (despite the partisan aims of the operation) and without any attempt to "push" voters, because many people will not give truthful answers to obviously partisan surveys. Many voters will refuse to participate, but if enough calls are made, a candidate or party can classify a critical mass of voters as supporters, opponents, undecideds, and nonvoters. Campaigns then can budget their scarce time and money by targeting persuasion efforts toward undecided voters—drawing on the issue-priority information gathered in the survey—and on turning out identified supporters on election day.

Such information is valuable to any campaign but was especially essential to me given the broken state of the local Democratic Party when I took over as chair in 1990. We had practically zero information of any value about voters in the district. In contrast to many other states, Minnesota has an open primary: one does not need to identify publicly with a particular party in order to vote in the primary. This meant we had no primary lists and thus no idea who the self-identified Democrats and Republicans were in the district. We had a few hundred names of Democratic caucus attendees over the past four years, but this was a miniscule fraction of the electorate and much smaller than the number of Democratic primary voters in the district. Moreover, a large proportion of past caucus attendees were MCCL affiliates who did not support the party's U.S. Senate candidate in 1990, nor its presidential candidate, nor me, in 1992.

The state DFL had even less information than I did about voters in the district. (The Bertram brothers had their own lists of supporters, but they did not share them with either the party or my campaign, and many of their supporters would not vote for other Democrats anyway.) The Republican Party might have encountered some of the same obstacles, though I suspect they had better local lists than our party did. But having a Republican incumbent in the district, and a candidate supported by an impressive extra-party network like the MCCL, meant that a pro-life Republican legislative candidate in our district faced smaller initial voter-information obstacles than I did. The only good lists we had were the ones I myself had generated as party chair during my two years of rebuilding, and the ones I was now assembling in my door-to-door campaigning. But some voters are more likely to reveal their true views in an impartially phrased phone survey than to a candidate at the door.

An effective phone survey operation, however, was very expensive, both in money (renting office space and installing multiple phone lines) and in the number of volunteer hours needed to staff it day in, day out in order to generate the necessary quantity of information. This would have been very difficult for a single legislative campaign to do on its own. The phone exchange grid in my district made it even harder: to call five miles away, say from Avon to Albany, was a long-distance call. We could ask our supporters to make phone calls but not to rack up hundreds of dollars in phone bills calling around the district. (Today, cell phones would make a phone bank operation by a single legislative campaign much less financially difficult than it was then, though the cost in volunteer hours remains unchanged.)

What we needed here was state party support. More specifically, we hoped my race would be "targeted" for the United Democratic Fund (UDF) phone survey effort. The UDF was a complicated intraparty consortium that operated phone banks in selected districts on behalf of the party's candidates for the legislature up to president. The UDF's phone script in 1992 began with the caller saying, "Hello, may I speak with ——? My name is —— and I'm calling for Voter Survey Research" (a fictitious name; the actual sponsor would be revealed at the end of the call if the respondent requested). If the respondent was willing to continue, the first question asked the individual which of a series of problems he or she considered most important (improving public education, reducing taxes, creating jobs, affordable health care, fighting crime, protecting the environment). Question two asked who the respondent was supporting for president; question three asked about congressional candidates (Collin Peterson and Bernie Omann in our district); question four about the state senate, naming whoever the Republican and Democratic candidates were (no other parties mentioned); question five did the same for the state house contest. Question six asked about abortion: do you consider yourself mainly pro-choice, mainly pro-life, or somewhere in between? Question seven asked whether respondents considered themselves Democrat, Republican, or independent. If they said "independent," there was a follow-up question asking whether they leaned Democratic or Republican. The final question was to verify the voter's name and address.

This survey generated accurate and valuable information without any partisan bias embedded in the questions. In this respect it differed from so-called push polls where if a respondent says he or she is undecided, the caller then follows with some damaging piece of alleged information about the opposition candidate to see if this changes the respondent's mind. Most voters can see through this kind of manipulation.

That is not what we wanted. We needed to find out as impartially as possible which voters were undecided and what issues they cared about so we could persuade them to support me, and who my decided supporters were so we could turn them out on election day. The list of undecided voters and their issue profiles was to be used in making persuasion calls. (Persuasion calls attempt to convince an undecided voter to support a candidate. They should be distinguished from calls designed to turn out already identified supporters.) We prepared campaign letters focused on each one of the issue areas named in the survey, so that if a voter listed health care as his or her highest priority, I could send out a health care–focused letter, and the same with education, job creation, and the other concerns.

But our strategy here depended on first acquiring the information, and this proved to be the bottleneck. It would have been extremely costly and an inefficient use of volunteer time for us to run such an operation for my legislative campaign alone. Moreover, I was running with, not against, the party's national ticket. We needed the resources of the UDF, and in exchange we were ready to contribute dozens of our own campaign volunteers to its effective operation.

The UDF's status as an in-kind campaign contribution meant that it was subject to some legal restrictions; for example, its operations had to support three or more party candidates, not just one. How and where the phone survey operation was deployed was dependent on the vagaries of intraparty politics. Decisions about which campaigns would or would not be "targeted" for this scarce and treasured resource were closely guarded and made through a process that was hidden from us.

Right after I announced my candidacy, Pia and I took a trip to visit with Democratic legislators and political operatives in St. Paul. We brought along a detailed campaign plan and made clear to anyone who would listen that we wanted my race UDF targeted. In this we were disappointed. I remember one meeting with a Democratic political operative who had begun looking into the electoral history (or what they call the DFL index) of the district. This includes not only legislative races but how the district voted in presidential, U.S. Senate, gubernatorial, and U.S. Representative contests. "We've processed the numbers, and they're not as bad as they look at first," she told me, intending this as encouragement.

I cannot blame her for her skepticism. The DFL legislative candidate in 1990 had received 32 percent of the vote. In 1988, when Bernie Omann faced his first reelection contest, a stronger DFL candidate received 41 percent of the vote. The district's voting results for the 1988 presidential race and the 1990 U.S. Senate race, the best indications of core Democratic support, were not encouraging at all. The 1992 redistricting had shifted the district farther in a Republican direction. Even making allowances for an open seat in 1992, these were not good numbers. They could be inflated by pretending that District 14 State Senator Joe Bertram's supporters were all staunch Democrats, but she knew and I knew this was false. Targeting my race would have looked to an independent observer at the beginning of the campaign like betting a lot of money on an unlikely horse.

Over time we were able to moderate the skepticism to a certain degree. But we were never able to convince statewide party operatives to assign my race anything higher than a midlevel priority. The caucus did steer some money my way (as I note in the next chapter), but from my perspective, that was less essential than the phone banks. Only late in the campaign, and to a frustratingly limited extent, were we permitted to do UDF calling in my district. We had large numbers of campaign volunteers ready and willing to call in District 14A. The phone surveys we were able to complete proved that the Read-Dehler race was close. This ought to have convinced party higher-ups to target fully my race. But our volunteers were permitted to call only the lists we were given, and the UDF never made call lists available to us for more than a small proportion of households in the district (and none that required long-distance calls from St. Cloud). The initial judgment of low priority was never revised.

To make matters worse, the UDF held on to survey information for months and only released it late in the campaign—in time to do get-out-the-vote calling but no real persuasion of undecided voters. This would have been an even greater obstacle were it not for our bending the rules a bit: we had our volunteers make a duplicate record of the information they generated through their own calls so that we had it immediately rather than waiting two months. (We cleared this with the local UDF staffer; toward higher-ups we employed a "don't ask, don't tell" policy.)

We also were able to compensate partly for the very limited number of UDF-allocated calls by employing the UDF script to make our own phone calls elsewhere in the district, using a registered voter list we purchased from the secretary of state's office. Our volunteers used their own phone lines or our campaign office phone. This was the only way we were able to do any calling in the western part of the district and in Morrison County (which would have been long-distance calls from the UDF office in St. Cloud). But it was a further drain on volunteer time, and the number of completed surveys could not compare to what would have been possible with a party-sponsored operation sporting a dozen phone lines from a single location.

The relatively small number of UDF calls we were permitted to make in District 14A, added to the surveys we did on our own, provided us with information on only a modest proportion of the ten thousand households (and roughly twenty-two thousand eligible voters) in the district. When we did have survey information on a particular voter, we sent him or her a letter detailing my position on whatever issue they had assigned highest priority. I personally called or visited every voter listed as undecided in my race, and of course in our get-out-the-vote efforts we called all persons who described themselves in the phone surveys as Jim Read supporters (see chapter 6).

We believed then and believe today that a good targeted phone operation might have turned the election in our favor. In her postelection report to the House DFL caucus, Pia wrote, "What we really needed, but did not get in any significant way, was phone banks to do UDF surveying. We sporadically were allowed two days a week in the St. Cloud Office but ran out of names (never re-supplied) at a crucial time. . . . *It is not possible for a Democrat to win this district without surveys.*"

What was uppermost in our minds during the campaign was the enormous value of phone survey information. What has increasingly struck me in the years since I ran for office, however, is the wide range of different — sometimes mutually incompatible — campaign strategies for which precise voter classification can be used. Simplifying somewhat, we can identify two basic strategies: a broadly targeted persuasion strategy and a narrowly targeted base strategy. Of course, all campaigns spend some resources both on persuading undecided voters and turning out identified supporters. But how a campaign allocates its scarce time and money among these two goals reveals its basic priorities and campaign philosophy.

Both strategies presuppose that through phone surveys, or in some other way, the campaign has acquired reliable information about supporters, opponents, undecided voters, people unlikely to vote, and so on, and the specific issues most likely to mobilize each individual voter. Both strategies presuppose that identified supporters will be diligently contacted and turned out on election day.

Where the two strategies differ is in how time and resources are used in the months preceding the final get-out-the-vote push. A persuasion strategy assigns roughly equal weight to mobilizing the base and to persuading undecided voters to swing your way. Self-described independents, and even some voters who affiliate with the opponent's party, may care about issues in ways that make them potentially persuadable. And even turning out the supposed party loyalists may require *re*-persuading voters for whom the party's message has lost vitality over time. In my own district, for example, the ravages of the abortion controversy over two decades meant I could not take for granted the votes of old-time Democrats (as the state and national party too often did); I often had to persuade them too. Persuasion was my campaign strategy, as a Democrat in a Republican district with a strong pro-life movement, and this was the reason I wanted phone survey information as early as possible. Persuasion takes time.

The "base" strategy puts less faith and resources in the attempt genuinely to persuade undecideds or voters leaning initially toward the opponent. Instead, more of the campaign's financial and time resources—throughout the campaign, not just in the final days—are directed toward identifying and mobilizing "the base": those voters who the campaign assumes already agree with the candidate or party and do not need to be persuaded. Fewer resources are put into persuading undecided voters during the long months leading up to election day. Instead, so-called swing voters might be the target of last-minute, emotionally laden appeals (often attack ads), whose persuasive effect evaporates soon but, the campaign hopes, just might last through election day.

No campaign deliberately spends resources trying to change the minds of committed opponents. What most distinguishes the persuasion from the base strategy is how they treat voters whose leanings are uncertain or about whom little information is available. (For instance, some voters might have recently moved into the district, or were not available to answer phone surveys, or refused to participate in them.) A campaign following a base-turnout strategy will ignore voters about whom it possesses no information—in some cases, preferring not even to remind them of the upcoming election.

I speak from experience here. Recently I participated in what was billed as a massive door-knocking campaign on behalf of the DFL candidate for a statewide office. I was somewhat surprised when on a long street with fifty or so houses, my door-knocking partner and I were given a list of three houses to visit. I was definitely instructed not to contact any households not on the list. This was, I was assured, a very carefully targeted list, and we were not to disrupt the campaign's strategy (which in the end proved unsuccessful). This bore little resemblance to the broadly directed door knocking I had practiced as a candidate for office.

These two competing strategies are not limited to Minnesota or to local and state races. In 2004 the Democratic presidential candidate John Kerry pursued a narrowly targeted 270 electoral vote strategy, which meant that little attempt was made to persuade a large percentage of the American population living in states where the presidential contest was not expected to be close. This strategy, of course, did nothing to help Democratic congressional candidates in states ignored by the Kerry campaign, and nothing to produce any new Democratic voters in those states. In the 2006 congressional election the Republicans followed a narrowly targeted turn-out-the-base strategy, now widely admitted to have been a mistake, while the Democrats, reversing course from 2004, successfully pursued what was now called a "fifty-state strategy."

My own perspective as a one-time candidate and local party chair is doubtless limited, and I do not pretend to know what works best for all candidates in all districts. Many candidates have run for office and won using narrowly targeted base-turnout strategies. But given the character and political history of my district, a persuasion strategy was my only option. I was running in the Minnesota equivalent of a "red-state" district. Any statewide party strategy that focused on turning out the base at the expense of persuading new supporters was one that wrote off my campaign and district from the outset. A base has to be *created* — and sometimes *re*-created — before it can be turned out.

As local party chair from 1990 to 1992, I had discovered how completely the Democratic base in our district had been eroded. This had occurred not because people in the community were indifferent to the party's bread-and-butter issues (support for public education, reforming health care, decent wages, economic fairness), but because the party and many of its national and statewide candidates had forgotten how to connect those issues to the lives and understanding of voters in our district. People come to understand and support a party or candidate's position on issues the same way they are persuaded to cast their vote: one individual conversation at a time.

CHAPTER FOUR

Dollars and Private Promises

On July 9, I officially filed with the secretary of state's office as a candidate for the Minnesota Legislature in District 14A. Soon afterward I began receiving dozens of questionnaires in the mail from, to name a few, the Minnesota Association of Professional Employees, the Minnesota Education Association, the International Brotherhood of Electrical Workers, the Teamsters, the Minnesota Chamber of Commerce, the Minnesota Association of Realtors, Minnesota Citizens Concerned for Life, the Abortion Rights Council of Minnesota, the Minnesota League of Conservation Voters, the National Rifle Association, the Minnesota Hospital Association. As a political scientist, I knew about the role of so-called special interest groups in our political process. But the sheer number, range, and specificity of groups took me by surprise. My attention was demanded by organizations claiming to represent the interests of doctors, nurses, nursing homes, dentists, dental hygienists, chiropractors, trial lawyers, schoolteachers, school boards, school principals, opticians, optometrists, ophthalmologists, township officers, city officers, police officers, hunters, women, children, the handicapped, the elderly, families, people without families, people planning families, people opposed to planning families — I could go on.

To a veteran legislator, the omnipresence of organized, politically interested groups must seem as ordinary and necessary as gravity. But to a first-time candidate, it more resembles some three-headed, thirty-eyed beast recently discovered in the Amazonian wilderness: not necessarily evil, not even especially dangerous, just very odd, and quite time-consuming to feed and manage.

The term *special interests* has stereotyped associations that inhibit understanding. *Politically organized groups* is a more accurate and neutral term. The special interest label implies that lobbyists and representatives of groups who communicate their concerns to legislators and candidates are somehow more selfish and less public-spirited than the rest of us. I do not believe this to be true.

It would be better to set aside our preconceived images and look with fresh eyes at the role of politically active groups in legislative campaigns. What most struck me in meeting all these groups for the first time was their *issue-explaining* and *commitment-demanding* character. Especially if you are a first-time candidate, these groups invite you to join them in an intense political conversation that, at its best, enhances the impact of the exchanges you have with voters at the door. But the corresponding danger is that conversations with groups might *substitute* for conversations with ordinary voters. Taken together, these organized groups constitute a kind of alternative public that is far better informed and more persuasive than the regular public you encounter at the doors. They seek out candidates and demand specific promises far more energetically than ordinary voters do. They also demand an enormous amount of the candidate's time when getting to thousands of households is difficult enough.

Many of these groups also contribute Political Action Committee money to the candidates they endorse. But I believe it is a mistake to categorize them simply as influence purchasers, and a narrow preoccupation with money misses what is most troubling about the interrelationship between groups and candidates. The principal problem is not the money. Campaigns must be paid for somehow, and at least PAC contributions are publicly disclosed. On matters of political money Minnesota is cleaner than most states, and angelic compared to what routinely takes place in Congress.

The problem is not the money per se but the fact that the specific written commitments a candidate makes to groups on their questionnaires are almost entirely hidden from the actual public. The public can discover that a particular group with an identifiable political agenda has contributed money to a candidate. But what has been specifically promised remains hidden. Public issues are transacted in the currency of private promises.

Where the Money Came From and Where It Went

Before I describe my private dialogues with this alternative public, it would help to sketch out the wider picture of campaign fund-raising and spending: how much money I spent, what I spent it on, and where it came from.

According to a postelection report we prepared for the Minnesota House DFL caucus, we spent a total of $20,600 on the campaign. (This is not the exact final figure, because there were a few postelection contributions and expenses.) Our spending was within the limit of $21,576 for the 1992 calendar year to which candidates had to agree to be eligible for public campaign funds. Our spending total worked out to $1.37 for every person who voted in the election.

Our largest single expenditure was on printed materials: $6,110. This included brochures I handed out at the doors, cards we distributed at parades, and direct mailings. We spent $3,630 on postage (plus $803 on envelopes), $3,085 on print ads in newspapers, and $3,004 on radio ads. There were no TV ads. Other expenditures included office rental for two months along with one phone line, gasoline, lawn signs, filing fee, T-shirts, and voter lists.

The sources of money were as follows: individual contributions, $6,034 (the largest single category); followed by PAC contributions, $4,596; the public campaign subsidy, $3,646; transfer contributions (mostly from "friends of" committees), $3,200; and party contributions, $2,138, most of that from the local party. This left a campaign debt of about $1,000, which we retired by getting some postelection contributions.

The expenditure we listed for gasoline, $241, seems low. I probably paid for the gas myself in the first half of the campaign and only began reimbursing myself later. In May 1993, I personally contributed $204.83 to pay the remaining campaign debt. Other than the partial gasoline subsidy, this final small payment, and a few incidentals, we did not fund the campaign out of our own pockets. This would have been impossible in any case, and I was against it on principle: running for public office should be open to anyone, wealthy or not. If people believe in you, they should be willing to fund your campaign.

In this respect the system worked, and I have no complaints. I did not have to spend inordinate amounts of my personal time soliciting campaign contributions (in stark contrast to congressional, senatorial, and presidential campaigns). The amount of money I spent, and the way I spent it, was about what was needed to communicate effectively with voters.

Much has been said about the "obscene amount of money" spent today on political campaigns in the United States.[1] I do not deny that in some cases campaign expenditures are indeed excessive and threaten the health of our democracy. But I do not think spending was excessive in my own campaign, nor in Minnesota legislative campaigns generally. I believe I spent essential dollars in appropriate quantities. Spending much less would have made it impossible for me as a first-time candidate to explain myself to voters; spending much more would have been overkill.

Easier Than I Expected

Like nearly every first-time candidate, I was very nervous about whether I could raise enough money. Our fund-raising target of $20,000 looked pretty daunting at a time when my annual income from teaching was just over $30,000. And I especially needed to raise *early* money from individual contributors living in the district. I had begun campaigning and spending money in March. My earliest PAC contributions did not arrive until August, and most of that pool of money came in September and October. My opponent (who was not wealthy either) took out a $3,400 personal loan to fund the early stages of his campaign; I was not willing to do this.

More importantly, raising a significant amount of early money from individual contributions would demonstrate that I was a stronger candidate than people thought. I was a recent transplant lacking roots in the community, I was perceived by many as "too liberal" for the district, and the pro-life groups — the strongest organized political force in the district — were against me. A weak start with fund-raising would have reinforced the skepticism and finished me off before the campaign even began. A strong early fund-raising performance would force people to take me seriously.

I did have one advantage over many first-time candidates. In my two-year stint as local Democratic Party chair I had overcome the distaste, the apologetic tone, and the misplaced guilt that many first-time candidates feel when they hit people up for political contributions.[2] In 1990 I had taken over a financially bankrupt party organization. To create a functional local party, I had to act on the principle that if people believe in your party's candidates, they should back it up with their pocketbooks. That principle did not change when I myself became the candidate. What did change, however, was the magnitude of the task: I would have to raise far more money from individual contributions in a shorter period of time than I ever did as party chair.

Raising the necessary campaign money turned out to be easier than I expected. Leaving aside for the moment the hours I spent filling out organized-group questionnaires—which served several purposes besides fund-raising—I never had to spend a large chunk of my time soliciting contributions. There were a number of reasons for this. The single most important factor was that friends, colleagues, and hitherto-discouraged local Democrats were delighted that they had a candidate they could enthusiastically support and contributed as soon as I asked them, sometimes before I asked. I also had some really effective fund-raisers among my volunteers—though no volunteer can raise much money if the candidate fails to generate enthusiasm. Minnesota's unique campaign contribution refund program (described later) helped speed the pace of individual contributions. Once I had built an impressive base of individual contributions, other forms of money, including transfer contributions and PAC money, flowed more freely. The public campaign subsidy was larger than I expected. So in the end only about a third of my campaign funds ($6,034) came from individual contributions, most of it that crucial early money. But I am convinced that with the help of Minnesota's campaign contribution refund program, I could have raised the entire campaign fund from individual contributions if I had had to.

An early incident helped me clarify my own approach to fund-raising by indicating a direction I did *not* want to go. As soon as I announced I was running for office, I began asking around for fund-raising advice. District 14B Representative Jeff Bertram (this was before the falling-out described in chapter 5) strongly recommended that for my first fund-raiser I hold a "lobbyist breakfast." The idea was to arrange a fund-raising gathering somewhere near the state capitol and invite all the full-time lobbyists. Breakfast worked best because it fit the lobbyists' schedules. But, Jeff explained, it did not matter how many lobbyists actually showed up for the breakfast. Many lobbyists when they received my invitation would decide it was a good idea to contribute to my campaign.

Jeff's advice was well-intended, and he was clearly recommending something that had worked well for him. There was nothing illegal about what he was proposing. But I was queasy about it from the beginning and never followed up. (I called John Brandl to get a second opinion on Jeff's proposal. John said, "If you're troubled by it, don't do it.")

What immediately troubled me was that if I took Jeff's advice, my very first fund-raising event would be held out of district and draw money from people who were not my prospective constituents. That seemed like bad symbolism, and the opposition could easily use it against me. Something else disturbed me, though it took a while before I could put my finger on it. It was the implicit message that "if you want to play, you have to pay." There was no reason in the world why lobbyists who had never met me and knew little about me should contribute to my campaign unless they believed that was my access price should I be elected. (We are not talking here about PACs who decided to support me after carefully examining my views; that came much later in the campaign and troubled me less.) And ethical considerations aside, I suspect many lobbyists would have laughed at the presumption of a first-time candidate in a difficult district hinting that they had better contribute early money to stay on my good side.

I decided instead to hold my first fund-raiser in the district, on April 29 at Jim Graeve's house in St. Joseph. This was the town where I lived and worked. Later that same evening on the other side of town the district party convention met and endorsed me as their candidate. The timing and location of the event signified that my fund-raising base would be made up of local DFL activists (many of the same people who were coming to town that night to endorse me), people with whom I worked (Jim's house is just down the street from the College of St. Benedict), and our friends and neighbors. Our special guest was Representative Dee Long, the Speaker of the Minnesota House. I liked and admired her and was honored by her attendance at my event.

In the letter I sent out for the April 29 reception I went out of my way to signal that people could contribute to my campaign in other ways than with their pocketbooks. I said in my letter: "But financial support is only one of the elements of a successful campaign. There are many other ways in which you can help: door-knocking, signs, phone calls, recommenda-tions to friends and neighbors, keeping me informed of issues and problems that affect your area. I would welcome any help of whatever kind you have the time and energy to offer." I included something similar in every fund-raising pitch I sent out over the course of the campaign. It was not that I felt any inhibition at this point about asking people for money who I knew could afford it; I had gotten over that long ago. But any candidate who generates genuine enthusiasm (and especially a Democratic candidate, given the demography of partisan affiliation) will find among his or her supporters a significant number of people who for one reason or another cannot easily afford even a $25 contribution. This group includes many college students, senior citizens who depend almost entirely on Social Security, and people who are at the moment "down on their luck." What these different categories of people have in common is that they have more time than money to contribute to a campaign, and as a candidate you want to draw on that resource. The last thing you want to do is add humiliation to financial stress by implying they are useless to you if they cannot contribute money.

Most of my supporters, however, could afford a contribution somewhere in the $25 to $100 range, and if you do the math, you can see why raising the money needed for a legislative campaign is not that difficult if people genuinely believe in you. Suppose for the moment that when you declare your intention to run for office, there are a hundred people who convincingly express their support. (If there are not a hundred people who want to see you win, you should not run.) Some of these will be personal friends, including friends of a different political persuasion who are willing to make an exception in your case; some will be coworkers or other professional associates who see qualities in you that they believe the political system needs; some will be people who have worked with you in some community or volunteer activity (and many prospective candidates will know more people in this context than I did as a recent transplant); some will be local political activists who share your party affiliation and just want to be assured that you are not going to embarrass them.

Suppose further that these hundred people have various incomes, but none are extremely wealthy or living in poverty. A third are readily able to contribute $100; a third, $50; and a third (let's say thirty-four of them), $25. All of these people realize you need money early on, and because many of them know you personally and encouraged you to run for office in the first place, they will feel guilty if you fall into deep personal debt as a result. So they will readily turn their verbal support into financial support as long as you are willing to ask. This adds up to $5,800 in early money, which is more than sufficient to jump-start a competitive campaign. And if they have contributed to you in April or May and you are obviously running an effective campaign, many of them will be willing and able to contribute again by September or October. And by that time—assuming your campaign is clearly effective and competitive—there will be potential new contributors who have met you in the course of the campaign itself and formed a good impression of you. Late in the campaign you will also begin receiving money from less-committed people who up till now have been hedging their bets. If a legislative candidate cannot raise money this way, it means he or she is a weak candidate.

We raised $1,475 in two hours at that first event, all in individual contributions of modest size, most of it from people living in or just outside my district. This convinced us that raising money from individual contributions would not be that difficult. By July 23, I had raised almost $4,000, none of it yet from PACs. By August 12, I had raised $6,500, only $700 of it at that point from PACs. On September 13 (after all candidates had filed their first required public disclosures), the *St. Cloud Times* reported that I had raised $8,178 compared to my opponent's $3,953. I had in fact outraised most of the legislative candidates in central Minnesota, including incumbents, and most of it was in individual contributions. I had clearly proved my point. Anyone who looked at these figures would have to take my campaign seriously.

A Model Program

In 1990 the Minnesota legislature created an innovative system of public campaign finance that I made full use of in my 1992 campaign. The Political Contribution Refund Program works like this. Every voting-age Minnesota citizen is allocated a refundable political contribution allowance of $50 (or $100 total for a married couple who files joint tax returns). The recipient of the contribution must be a candidate for state office or some unit of a Minnesota political party. The recipient's treasurer provides a receipt, which the individual contributor sends to the Department of Revenue; two months or so later the contributor receives the refund, which comes out of the state's general fund. The $50 per person is a total for all contributions; thus, you could contribute $50 to one candidate, or give $25 apiece to two candidates, or $10 to five candidates, and so on. Any dollar contributed above the $50 per person allocation is not refundable.

The other side of the coin is that if candidates want to be eligible to receive these refundable individual contributions, they have to agree to spending limits. For Minnesota House campaigns in 1992, candidates who wanted to receive refundable contributions had to agree to spend no more than $21,576. Both my opponent and I agreed to these limits and participated in the refund program.

The U.S. Supreme Court ruled in *Buckley v. Valeo* (1976) that mandatory limits on campaign spending are unconstitutional. But voluntary spending limits with incentives to participate (like Minnesota's campaign refund) are still permissible. Many types of public campaign finance in the United States (including presidential election matching funds) function through voluntary incentives.

What makes the Minnesota program different is that each individual citizen gets to decide where his or her $50 allocation of public campaign funds will go. In most public campaign finance programs (including Minnesota's previously existing program, which remained on the books) the public campaign subsidy goes directly to the candidate, and only to candidates or parties deemed competitive enough to merit the money. Small parties and independent candidates understandably complain that such a system is rigged in favor of the major parties.

In Minnesota's new system, in contrast, a candidate must persuade individuals to pay money out of pocket and wait two months or so to get it back. So it is the individual contributor, not any state agency, who decides which candidate(s) deserve his or her public quota of money. Any candidate from any party, and even a candidate running without party affiliation, can receive refundable contributions as long as he or she agrees to the spending limits. Because individuals still have to advance money out of pocket and wait months for the refund, contributions do not flow in as effortlessly as one might suppose. A candidate still has to generate enthusiasm, or people will not part with their money, even temporarily. An individual who does not support your candidacy or is relatively indifferent to you is not going to give you money anyway, refund or no refund. An individual who genuinely supports you will be predisposed to contribute to your campaign anyway, refund or no refund—and many contribute again after they have used up their refundable quota. But my hunch based on personal experience as candidate and party chair is that the program speeds up the pace at which contributions come in, somewhat increases their magnitude, and reduces the amount of time a candidate personally has to spend persuading individuals to contribute.[3]

This last effect is especially valuable and is overlooked if we fixate only on how the Minnesota program affects total raising and spending. The same aggregate amount of money raised and spent will have very different consequences if under one set of rules raising the money requires an enormous investment of candidate time repeatedly to sweet-talk the ideologically committed, while under another set of rules the candidate, by raising the same money more quickly, can spend more time interacting with undecided voters at the door. I consider the latter an important goal and believe our campaign finance rules should deliberately promote it.

What complicates the picture in Minnesota is that the Political Contribution Refund Program was added to the old system of public campaign subsidies, when in my view it should have completely replaced it. The coexistence of two programs clouds the more principled character and example-setting potential of the new one. The older campaign subsidy program provided me with a total of $3,646, and I was not so principled as to send it back. But it should have been zero; all public campaign money, in my view, should come in the form of individual contributions.

No system of public campaign finance is perfect, and many attempted reforms (presidential campaign matching funds, for example) fail to live up to their promise. Despite the obstacles, I strongly support the idea of public campaign finance. Political money is not just political speech (as was assumed in the *Buckley v. Valeo* decision); it is also political power. Unequal wealth translates into unequal power over elections in a democracy where every citizen is supposed to enjoy an equal vote. Public campaign finance attempts to place reasonable limits on the political clout of unequal wealth and to remind officeholders they owe their election to ordinary voters, not just their own fortune or their biggest contributors. And if that is the goal, then I believe Minnesota's political contribution refund is the best model available.

Transfers and "Friends"

Another pool of campaign money came to me in the form of transfers from the campaign funds of Democratic legislators who had raised more money than they needed for their own campaigns. These transfers came in two different forms, which I did not clearly distinguish at the time. One type was a contribution from a legislator's own campaign fund. Thus, our October report lists a contribution of $300 from the Welle Volunteer Committee. Allen Welle was at that time majority leader of the Minnesota House. But I also received a contribution of $250 from the Friends of the House Majority Leader, a separate fund known as a "leadership PAC"; I also received $250 from Friends of the House Speaker, another leadership PAC.

Leadership PACs were later prohibited in Minnesota, in 1993, though they are still permitted in many states and in Congress. They raise ethical issues of which I was frankly oblivious at the time. In 1992 they were still legal and, from a first-time candidate's point of view, a helpful source of easy money. If I thought about them at all, I considered them a promising sign that someone in the caucus had faith in my campaign. I was more grateful for the symbolic expression of support than for the money itself.

But there are better ways in which the party leadership can signal its confidence in a new candidate. When an individual or a regular PAC contributes to a campaign, the source of the money is transparent. Leadership PACs defeat this goal of transparency: when I received these funds, I had no idea who had originally given this money to the leadership PAC or for what purpose. They are also a potential source of undue influence within the caucus. Newly elected candidates might feel themselves "in debt" to the legislator who provided the most funds—though neither Welle nor House Speaker Dee Long ever hinted that there were any strings attached to the funds they sent my way.

The money was so easy that at one point I went about seeking more of it. Someone—I do not remember who—suggested that I write to Democratic legislators with safe seats who held key leadership positions and ask them to contribute to my campaign. This pitch did not raise much money, and it was never an important fund-raising strategy. Some legislators did not reply; some replied that they could not spare money from their own campaigns; a few contributed from their campaign funds; a few made individual contributions from their own pockets.

But by far the most interesting response came from Representative Kathleen Vellenga, chair of the House Judiciary Committee. In a letter dated August 17, she wished me well in my campaign but declined to make a transfer contribution because she believed the whole system of transfers created conflicts of interest. If some PAC wants to support a campaign, she said, it should contribute directly, "rather than have those of us who are committee chairs (and thus more in a position for potential conflict of interest) becoming conduits. The latter has the potential for becoming 'gratitude all 'round'—the committee chairs to the PACs and the new candidates to the committee chairs."

As judiciary chair she must have been especially attuned to the danger of conflicts of interest and undue influence. I had unwittingly stumbled upon an argument taking place within the DFL caucus itself about which I was previously clueless. I understood her point immediately, felt chastened, and made no more pitches for transfer contributions.

The Questionnaires

Organized advocacy groups were the source of the blizzard of questionnaires I received during the campaign. What follows is not intended as simply another denunciation of the pernicious role of "special interest" money in politics. Countless books and articles have been written on that theme, and there is little new I could add. Having narrowly lost the election, I was never in a position to observe directly how political money shapes the legislative process itself.

Moreover, a narrow focus on PAC money fails to explain why many candidates spend substantial amounts of time answering questionnaires from groups who the candidate knows will not be contributing PAC funds to his or her campaign. In my own case, for example, I filled out questionnaires from the Minnesota Citizens Concerned for Life (MCCL), the National Rifle Association, and the Minnesota Chamber of Commerce, all of whom I knew would not be sending any money my way. There is another dimension to the story, one that tends to be overlooked in accounts preoccupied with money. A candidate's interaction with a politically organized group is at its best a serious conversation about important public issues — but one that takes place almost entirely out of public view. That is the troubling part. The money is secondary.

This side of the story is perhaps most evident to a first-time candidate struggling to master an enormous range of issues in a short time. A seasoned incumbent would probably take a much more detached attitude toward these groups and their questionnaires. But as a first-time candidate you are looking for support — and I do not just mean money — wherever you can find it, and you want to explain yourself to everyone. In most cases the questions the groups ask are fair ones, and you feel they are entitled to an answer or at least a promise to learn more about the matter. Moreover, these groups can be very helpful in explaining their legislative agenda to first-time candidates, who are struggling to master a huge range of complicated issues on top of all the other time demands of the campaign.

At their best these conversations supplement the issue discussions you have with voters in your district. As a rookie candidate you are extremely pressed for time, and it takes an enormous investment of time to reach thousands of voters at the door. Most voters will not come to you; you have to go to them. Unlike the voters, PACs and advocacy groups come to you. When you are struggling to learn the issues, this appears to save you time, and you can get down to business immediately without first having to make small talk about the weather. But the corresponding risk is that these conversations might *take the place* of conversations with your electorate. To a busy candidate, PACs and advocacy groups can easily morph into a kind of three-dimensional, full-spectrum hologram of the actual public. The remedy to this problem, I believe, is to make these quasi-public conversations genuinely public.

Here are a few examples from questionnaires. Some questions were very straightforward, while others were posed at a level of specificity and detail that was puzzling for a first-time candidate. Questionnaires typically had a dozen or so questions, sometimes more. In some cases submission of the completed questionnaire was followed by invitation to an in-person endorsement interview with representatives of the group; in other cases there was just the written questionnaire.

The Minnesota Elementary School Principals' Association asked: "Do you believe that class size makes a difference in student achievement at the elementary school level?" and "Do you agree that mandated programs should carry funding for their implementation?" I answered "yes" to both questions. There were some less transparent questions: "Do you agree that the present per pupil formula of .5 (kindergarten students), 1.0 (elementary students), and 1.35 (secondary students) used in funding our schools should be eliminated so that all students are counted equally under the foundation aid formula?" To this one, I wrote in the margin, "Undecided—need more information." (They endorsed me despite my hedging on this one.)

The Minnesota Association of Realtors asked some questions that were irritatingly general, such as: "Would you support legislation to cut spending?" (I answered "yes" to this one because I am certain I would have supported spending cuts on *something*.) It also asked some questions that were excruciatingly detailed, such as: "Would you author or support legislation to prohibit or restrict a real estate company affiliated with a title company from referring business 'in house' if the existing federal and state laws requiring disclosure and prohibiting kickbacks (RESPA & MN Stat. 92.19(3)) were satisfied?" To this I could only answer, "Need more information."

The Minnesota Chamber of Commerce had a very clear and aggressive political agenda. "Will you support consistency with Federal environmental mandates and only support more stringent terms in Minnesota environmental laws when the majority of scientific research supports different standards?" I was being asked, in other words, to promise not to raise Minnesota environmental standards above whatever minimum was established by the federal government. To this I answered "no" and went on to explain: "The character of Minnesota is special. Our natural environment is *better* than most other states and we should keep it that way."

I gave them a "yes" on support for workers' compensation reform. The Minnesota Chamber endorsed my opponent, as I expected.

The Minnesota Chiropractic Association began its questionnaire by asking whether I had every received chiropractic care myself ("no"), and whether I knew any chiropractors living in my district whom I could call on for advice on policy matters. To this I answered "yes" because I had recently had a long doorstep conversation with a chiropractor who had offered to make himself available for exactly this purpose. The questionnaire then proceeded to the association's legislative agenda, most of which was concerned with making sure chiropractors were not shut out of the health care reform process in Minnesota. I had a follow-up in-person meeting with a representative of the association, who explained to me at length what chiropractors do and how the chiropractic profession understands its own niche in the medical field as a whole. I found all of this helpful, and I supported their request to be included in health care policy discussions. Nevertheless they endorsed my opponent and contributed to his campaign.

The United Auto Workers questionnaire asked me what make and model cars I owned. (I was politically correct for both cars: a 1987 Chevy Celebrity and a 1968 Ford LTD.) They asked, "Do you believe companies should have the right to replace striking workers?" to which I answered "no" and added: "I support legislation that outlaws permanent replacement of striking workers." This was a big issue for the workers at the Champion paper mill in my district, which had recently had some fierce labor disputes. The UAW also asked, "Are there any needed changes on Workers' Compensation Law?" I answered "yes," which was the same answer I gave the Chamber of Commerce. Just in case all these answers became public—which never happened—I did not want to be caught saying one thing to one group and the opposite to another.

The two most time-demanding questionnaires (at least for me) came from the League of Conservation Voters and the Sierra Club, but I did not mind, because I had highlighted environmental issues in my campaign literature and I hoped to be a leader in this field once elected. The League's first question was, "What do you see as the top priorities for Minnesota in the area of environment and natural resources protection?" In my reply I talked about groundwater protection (a major concern within my district), protection of wetlands, encouraging energy conservation and development of alternative energy sources, and encouraging sustainable agricultural practices (threatened by recent budget cuts to the Minnesota Agricultural Extension Service). The Sierra Club asked, "What would you as a legislator do in order to protect biodiversity?" and "List some things you have done to show your commitment to environmental protection." My very detailed answers to both questionnaires were massive overkill: there was not a chance in the world these groups would endorse my opponent. But filling out the questionnaires helped me think through what kind of legislator I wanted to be if I won the election.

If you take the questionnaires seriously, as I did, and attempt to give responsible and realistic answers to questions, it very quickly becomes a huge time commitment. There are several ways in which a candidate might succeed in spending far less time on questionnaires than I did. One is to have someone fill out the questionnaires for you. In this case, of course, the educational value of the questionnaires is zero, and someone else will be committing you to a wide range of promises that you might not discover until later. A second time-efficient strategy would be to say "yes" to everything a group wants, without agonizing over any exceptions or qualifications. I was unwilling to do this even with the groups that ultimately endorsed me, because I felt it would compromise my independence. Moreover I believed—incorrectly, it turns out—that the press might take an interest in candidates' questionnaire answers and broadcast them to the world, and I did not want to say anything I would not want to see on the front page.

A third time-efficient strategy is to follow your party's legislative caucus (or your state party's) recommended answers to these questionnaires. The Minnesota House DFL caucus sent out "cheat sheets" that included recommended text for answering the questionnaires of especially important groups, and I assume my opponent's caucus did the same. I consulted these cheat sheets but did not depend on them. For one thing, the answers seemed to be keyed to Twin Cities districts, where Democrats typically did well, not to rural and small-town Stearns and Morrison counties.

(Furthermore, as a teacher, I am against plagiarism, even when it is done with permission.)

A final time-saving strategy is simply to refuse to answer any questionnaires and throw them all out. I have heard of candidates who do this or swear they will do it the next time they run, but they are usually either safe incumbents or challengers with no chance of winning anyway. I believe I could have run a competitive campaign without PAC money, but I do not think I could have thumbed my nose at the entire range of political advocacy groups. I could not afford to be falsely portrayed as an inveterate enemy of a group's concerns. I wanted to send the message that I was willing to listen even if we did not agree. It was the same message I believed I was sending when I went to the door of someone I knew would not vote for me.

In retrospect, however, I clearly spent more time than was necessary answering questionnaires and meeting with representatives of advocacy groups. It is easy to exaggerate the degree to which these organized groups can help or hurt your campaign. They make enormous demands on your time and energy when both are very scarce. And in the end only the voters of the district can elect you.

Public Issues and Private Promises

This vast system of questionnaires and screenings is not limited to Minnesota nor to state legislative elections. It is widespread across the United States. But there seems to be no general agreement on the status of the answers candidates give on written questionnaires. In answering questionnaires, should candidates be seen as taking public positions on public issues? Or are they engaging in privileged communications like those between a lawyer and a client? Some groups explicitly state that questionnaire answers are confidential, though it is unlikely that they could legally prohibit a candidate from publicizing them. Occasionally the ambiguous status of questionnaires becomes a campaign issue. In a 2002 legislative campaign in New Hampshire the challenger called for both candidates to release publicly their answers to group questionnaires, arguing that "everything should be out in the open" and that the questionnaires are "used to get candidates to say things during their most vulnerable time." The incumbent refused to release her questionnaires on the grounds that her answers were the intellectual property of the groups posing the questions. In a 2006 legislative campaign in Tennessee the challenger posted all of his questionnaire answers on his campaign Web site.[4] I suspect one could find this same dispute arising in many campaigns in many states.

What is also unclear is whether in answering questionnaires a candidate is understood to be making promises or merely expressing a non-binding opinion. At the beginning of my own campaign I read or was told by someone — this may have come from the House DFL caucus — that questionnaire answers are not pledges but merely expressions of one's current thinking on some matter. And in my records I did find at least one questionnaire, the one from the Abortion Rights Council of Minnesota, which prefaced its questionnaire with the assurance that "Your answers to these general questions will NOT be interpreted as PROMISES for votes on specific bills but are only statements of your present thinking." But most groups do not include any such disclaimer. More typical is the approach of the pro-life group the Minnesota Citizens Concerned for Life, which prefaces its questionnaire with the statement (underscored in the original for emphasis) that *"On every question below, a 'yes' response indicates agreement with the position of Minnesota Citizens Concerned for Life."* The tone here clearly signals a binding commitment. The MCCL then uses its questionnaire answers as ammunition in its independent-expenditure campaign materials; my own questionnaire answers were used this way. It is not much of a reply to say, "That only reflected my thinking at the time."

Speaking from experience as a first-time candidate in a close race, answering the questionnaires does not feel like a snapshot of your current thinking. It feels like you are making a commitment. If it merely reflected your current thinking, there would be nothing preventing you from telling every group exactly what it wants to hear and then ignoring it the next day, in which case the whole process would be pointless. And many groups certainly treat questionnaire answers as commitments, especially if they are contributing PAC money or urging their members to campaign actively for their endorsed candidate. I know of several cases where legislators have been taken to task by groups for acting or voting differently than they indicated to the group during their most recent campaign.

The campaign contribution a PAC makes to an endorsed candidate is a matter of public record. What a candidate says to groups in written questionnaires should also be public record. (Oral follow-up conversations between group and candidate that are not audiotaped or videotaped raise somewhat different issues, and I do not insist on making them public.) If I were to run for office again, I would post my questionnaire answers on the Web, challenge my opponent to do the same, and urge the press (whose coverage of legislative campaigns is sometimes abysmally superficial) to make questionnaire answers a regular element of campaign coverage for offices at every level.

For example, the first question on the 1992 MCCL legislative questionnaire was, "Would you vote for a law that would prevent abortions, other than to prevent the death of the mother?" The MCCL's own membership is told candidates' answers to this question. Shouldn't the public as a whole know this as well? For there are cases where candidates have gotten away with a double game on hot-button issues, sending one message to an advocacy group and another to the general public. Among other advantages, publicizing questionnaires would allow the press, without any great expenditure of time, to report on campaigns in greater depth and on a wider range of issues than they currently do.

My proposal to make questionnaires public does not proceed from the assumption that "special interests" are pernicious and need to be "exposed." I suspect there are cases of backroom deals that would not withstand public scrutiny, and of course here the rationale for public disclosure is obvious. But I never observed anything like this. The representatives of PACs and advocacy groups I met, even the ones that actively opposed me, were public-spirited men and women passionately concerned about public issues. Some of the questionnaire items were extremely narrow and oriented to legislative insiders; I have given a few examples, and I could supply many more. But many questions were fair, appropriate, and directed toward important public concerns.

But this is simply another reason why candidates' written promises to

PACs and other advocacy groups should be public. When as a candidate I described my environmental priorities for the state, why should the audience be limited to the League of Conversation Voters? When I said I opposed hiring permanent replacements for striking workers, why should only the unions hear this? The scarce campaign time a candidate expends answering questionnaires would perhaps be justified if he or she is understood to be working out public positions on public issues. For in this case the public itself benefits from an educational process spurred by a questionnaire. But if in answering questionnaires candidates are merely making private communications to a group, I do not believe it merits the time expenditure.

During the Progressive Era of U.S. history, reformers often invoked the image of a virtuous public shining light into the suspicious darkness of special interests.[5] But my own experience as a candidate suggests a rather different metaphor, that of a diversion channel: a less-than-fully-informed public is deprived of the nourishing stream of public discourse that competitive campaigns ought to provide, because that stream has been drawn off in another direction — into these intense but nonpublic conversations between candidates and organized groups.

Candidate conversations with advocacy groups at their best enhance wider public discussions. But they also risk driving out genuinely public discussions. Meetings with advocacy groups can easily look and feel to a candidate like meetings with a surrogate public. This substitution is especially likely to happen when time is short, voters are elusive, the press is inattentive, and advocacy groups are so well-informed and persuasive.

CHAPTER FIVE

Abortive Dialogue

On July 15 when I was door-knocking in the town of Holdingford, I flagged down a man mowing his lawn who seemed to be in his late sixties. He turned out to be an old-time Democrat who had once been active in local campaigns. He used to own a hog farm but now lived here in town. We talked about the condition of the roads, the strengths and weaknesses of past Democratic legislative candidates, and other things. He seemed to like me immediately, and I liked him. He spontaneously pulled out his wallet and gave me a $20 campaign contribution in cash. I sent him a follow-up note thanking him for the conversation and the contribution. I was counting on him to put in a good word for me with his friends and neighbors in Holdingford.

A couple of months later he called me on the phone. The Minnesota Citizens Concerned for Life (MCCL) had sent out a newsletter to its members listing candidates' answers to their legislative questionnaire. (I do not remember if he was a member himself or had received the information from someone else.) He was very troubled by my answers and went over the questionnaire with me point by point. I had given the MCCL a "yes" on eight items, a "no" on eight items, and left a few unanswered. He was especially concerned about my "no" answer to the question: "Would you support legislation or amendments which would prohibit government funding of abortion except in those cases necessary to prevent the death of the mother?" I gave him my standard explanation (which I had also written onto the questionnaire sheet) that whatever restrictions we make regarding abortion must apply equally to rich and poor; the rightness or wrongness of an abortion shouldn't depend on how it is paid for. He was not persuaded by my explanation of this or any of my other "no" answers. He kept saying, "Jim, this just doesn't look good." His tone was not one of accusation or condemnation but rather of sadness. He said he could not support me.

I said I respected his decision. I then asked him if he wanted his $20 contribution back. He replied that he had completely forgotten about it, but now that I had mentioned it, yes, he did want me to return the contribution. I sent it back to him along with a letter in which I said I still hoped he would choose to vote for me. I never spoke with him again before the election, and not long after the election he died. On election day I did not do well in Holdingford, despite its being one of the few traditionally Democratic-leaning towns in the district.

Attempt at a Dialogue

During my campaign for the Minnesota Legislature I tried to find some principled middle position on the abortion issue in a district where pro-life absolutists had hitherto enjoyed a political lock hold. In addition to setting forth my own position, I genuinely sought to encourage dialogue on abortion in place of the "dialogue of the deaf" or "clash of absolutes" that many people consider inevitable. I did not realistically expect that my own position statement on the issue (which I will discuss later) would be written into law. It reflected my personal views on abortion; voters had a right to know what these were regardless of their probability of being enacted. More importantly, my position statement, and everything I said on the subject orally or in writing during the campaign, was intended as a conversation opener: to get beyond the fixed positions and standard rationales that continually reproduced this dialogue of the deaf.

The title of this chapter is an admission that my success in this effort was at best limited. But I do not consider it a failure. If I had won the election by a convincing margin in a district where no legislative candidate had run, much less won, on anything other than absolute opposition to abortion, the experiment could have been pronounced a success. If I had been blown out, as most people expected, my experiment would have been a clear failure. The actual result—a loss close enough to require a recount—suggests at least limited success, but readers will have to draw their own conclusions.

I did not run for office for the purpose of conducting a six-month experiment on the possibility of genuine abortion dialogue. On the contrary, the abortion issue was the biggest reason for me *not* to run, and I would have sidestepped the issue if I could. But that was impossible. I sought dialogue because given my own views and the character of the district, I had no other choice.

When people think about abortion as a national debate, they typically think of two camps of equally vocal activists confronting one another, with the rest of the American public caught in between. A common visual image often captured in photographs is of rival pro-choice and pro-life demonstrations in front of the U.S. Supreme Court building, face-to-face and shouting at one another.

But this visual image did not describe the district in which I was running. The appropriate image in my district would be of one side, the pro-life side, demonstrating and shouting at deafening levels, and the pro-choice side completely silent and hiding in the shadows. I myself was genuinely torn on the issue, like much of the American public. But under the special circumstances of my district I became the "pro-choice extreme" because I was the lone campaign voice willing to offer publicly any alternative to the absolute prohibitionists, and because I openly challenged the political power of the MCCL, which considered the district its own.

Never in the course of the campaign did I say, "A woman has a right to do with her body whatever she chooses." Instead, all of my statements on the issue presupposed that abortion was bad but denied that criminal prohibition was the appropriate response, instead favoring other methods of bringing abortion rates down. Whenever someone was willing to hear me out, I would compare abortion to war: war is an evil too, I would say, but that does not mean I can make it disappear from the planet by passing a law against it.

The opinion polls conducted by Steve Frank, a political scientist at St. Cloud State University, showed that opinion on abortion in Stearns County generally mirrored the state and nation as a whole. My district was a few percentage points further in the pro-life direction than the statewide mean, but the differences were not dramatic, and the absolute prohibitionist position pushed by the MCCL was supported by only a small minority.

But it is well understood among political scientists that an organized and committed minority is often more powerful than an unorganized and less committed majority, and the MCCL was far better organized and more passionately committed than anyone else in the district.

Occasionally in the course of the campaign I would meet people who identified themselves as clearly pro-choice: usually privately, less often publicly, and in numbers far smaller than the other side's public self-identification. What this meant, if Frank's poll numbers were accurate, was that at least in my district, pro-lifers were vocal and pro-choicers were quiet. I believe most pro-choice people voted for me as the lesser of two evils, assuming they did not strongly disagree with me on some other issue. Unlike pro-choice activists in the Twin Cities, who can be as single-issue and absolutist as their pro-life counterparts, pro-choicers in my district knew what I was up against.

I believed I was accomplishing something important simply by voicing publicly an alternative to the pro-life absolutist position. The absolute pro-lifers did not just criticize my position as morally wrong. They also said to me, in effect, "How *dare* you go door-to-door in our community saying things like that!" The battle was as much about freedom of speech in local political campaigns as it was about abortion.

An Attempt at Middle Ground

Pia and I wrote up the following statement early in the campaign, before I had publicly announced my candidacy, and I stuck to it throughout. I did not include it in my regular campaign brochure but instead handed it out or summarized it verbally whenever anyone asked my position on the issue. We titled it "The Abortion Controversy: A Search for Common Ground."

> I favor outlawing abortion after the twelfth week of pregnancy except in severe circumstances such as to save the life of the mother. But I also believe that legal sanctions by themselves do very little to solve the problems that lead to abortion. Abortion can be much more effectively prevented through education, adoption counseling, and after-birth support. We must also work

to change a society in which sexual violence against women is commonplace, and a media culture that encourages teenagers to behave in irresponsible ways.

I believe that officeholders and candidates for office should search for some practical common ground on this controversy that threatens to paralyze our public life. Even those who disagree about when human life begins should be able to work together to reduce the number of abortions that occur. If elected, I would work with anyone who can offer a realistic and humane solution to the problem of abortion in our state and our nation.

The central messages of the statement were (1) that abortion was bad, but there were better ways to reduce its incidence than an absolute and unenforceable ban; and (2) that people with very different moral and theological views ought to be able to find some "practical common ground" in supporting measures that reduced the abortion rate. Here was my call for dialogue in place of the clash of absolutes. In saying this I was signaling a willingness to talk with and listen to even the MCCL. Whether they desired any dialogue with me remained to be seen.

Readers will notice here that my position was more restrictive than the *Roe v. Wade* Supreme Court decision. *Roe* (and its many follow-up rulings) held that abortion could be subjected to severe restrictions after viability (about six months into a pregnancy). I was in effect proposing to shift this line from six months to three. Abortions rights activists might be quick to label my position "anti-choice" and perhaps see no essential difference between my position and that of the MCCL. But in the community in which I was campaigning, to affirm that women should have access to safe, legal abortion in the first trimester of pregnancy was a radical act.

In 1992 it was very unlikely that the U.S. Supreme Court would in the foreseeable future revise its abortion rulings enough to permit the twelfth-week restriction I was proposing, and if it did, the Minnesota legislature was unlikely to enact it. The absolute prohibition demanded by the MCCL was even more unlikely to be enacted, and its members, or at least the politically more sophisticated ones, knew this. Their immediate legislative hopes were targeted toward enacting restrictions on abortion at the margin (informed consent, parental consent, prohibition of public funding), all the while making clear that their ultimate goal was complete prohibition.

For this reason, people might wonder why I did not simply respond to the issue by saying, "The Supreme Court has decided this," or "Prohibition is just not going to happen." I did make that point on occasion. But to rely on that as my main argument would have been rightly seen as a cop-out. Voters had a right to know where I stood. The political effectiveness of the MCCL and comparable pro-life groups across the nation comes from their clearly announced moral position. It is not unreasonable to expect your local community's legislators to articulate a moral stance on abortion at the state capitol, whether or not that stance is likely to be enacted into law in the foreseeable future. My abortion statement was designed to offer a *different* moral stance than the one articulated by the MCCL. If voters elected me, it would mean that our rural and small-town, largely Catholic community would be sending to St. Paul a different moral message than their elected leaders had in the past. So there was a lot at stake here despite the unlikelihood that either the MCCL's position or mine would become law.

A veteran Democratic legislator from another central Minnesota district (not either of the Bertrams) read my statement carefully and told me he really liked it. He was one of the many out-state, pro-life Democrats in the legislature. He said to me, "I wish I could say what you are saying. But it's too late, I've boxed myself in."

Would my position on abortion have been different if I had been a candidate in a district friendlier to the pro-choice argument? It certainly would have been phrased differently: my actual statement was clearly directed toward people who considered abortion to be morally wrong.

But at its core the statement reflected my personal views on the issue, then and now. I considered abortion a tragedy, not a medical act comparable to removing a gall bladder. I was troubled by the prospect of late-term abortions, and if abortions were going to occur, the earlier in the pregnancy they occurred the better. I knew that most abortions happened before the twelfth week of pregnancy (the pro-life camp also pointed this out in their attacks on my position), but I also believed that middle- and late-term abortions, however uncommon, were only justifiable where something had gone seriously wrong with a pregnancy.

And I was serious about encouraging dialogue on prevention, however utopian this may sound. For example, generous medical and financial support for women *after* the child is born (instead of a passionate concern for fetuses that ends as soon as the umbilical cord is cut) seemed to me something on which pro-choicers and pro-lifers ought to be able to agree: the former because it improves the real choices available to a woman or teenage girl faced with an unplanned pregnancy, the latter because it might lead to fewer abortions. The MCCL legislative questionnaire was silent on the question of providing support to children and their mothers. But over the course of the campaign I did speak with many people morally opposed to abortion who completely agreed with me about the importance of supporting mothers and children. This was especially true of Catholics infused with a social justice ethic. And it should not be forgotten that I was teaching at a Catholic college sponsored by a Catholic Benedictine monastery.

The reader may recall from chapter 1 that Andy Blauvelt, who knew a lot about Minnesota politics, warned us that as an untenured faculty member I could jeopardize my job by running for office on anything short of a 100 percent pro-life platform. The Catholic Church teaches that abortion is wrong in all cases except to save the life of the mother. I was not Catholic, and our faculty handbook grants us academic freedom. But handbooks are not infallible protections. We will see later in the chapter that some of my pro-life opponents did try to make an issue of my teaching at a Catholic college. If I was going to lose my College of St. Benedict position for exercising my right to run for office I did not want to teach there. But it turns out this was a battle I did not have to fight.

Early in the campaign I met with Sister Colman O'Connell, the president of the College of St. Benedict, to talk about my candidacy. I described to her in some detail my own position on abortion and gave her a copy of my written statement. I was not asking her permission to take the stance I did on abortion. But it was only fair to alert her to the pressures pro-life activists in the community might put on her and the college. I emphasized I would make clear that my views as a candidate did not represent those of the College of St. Benedict; I knew she would insist on that point. If there was going to be an abortion battle, I wanted myself, not the college, to be the target. I did not mention the College of St. Benedict by name in my campaign literature, though where I worked was no secret.

She seemed to be satisfied with my explanation, because we spent the remaining forty-five minutes talking about financial aid and other prospective legislation affecting private colleges and universities in Minnesota. She seemed pleased at the prospect that the college might have one of its own representing us in St. Paul. We had several more political conversations over the course of my campaign, and I know she followed it closely, but the abortion issue never came up again. If pro-life activists among the community, alumni, or contributors were complaining to her about my stance on abortion, she never said anything to me about it. The prospective threat to my job never materialized. For that I am grateful.

Pro-lifers at the Door

The abortion issue arose in the course of my door knocking in a completely different manner than any other topic. My campaign literature invited conversations about health care and education and several other key issues. But I made no mention of abortion in my standard brochure. When abortion came up, it was always the voter at the door who initiated the discussion. And the committed pro-lifers considered it their duty to always bring it up whenever a candidate appeared at the door. In such cases abortion was usually the first and often the only topic of conversation.

A typical encounter with a committed pro-lifer would go like this. I would introduce myself and get through as much of my standard opening as the person was polite enough to permit. Then he or she would immediately ask, "Are you pro-life?" This was phrased as a question that permitted only one of two clear and obvious answers, "yes" or "no." I would refuse the "yes or no" alternative and instead either hand them my written statement or begin to explain it verbally. But often I was cut off after the second word because from their perspective any reply except the single word "yes" counted as a "no."

Sometimes the question was contracted to a single word: "Pro-life?"

Sometimes the vocal intonation of the single word suggested a period rather than a question mark: "Pro-life." Here the person was showing where he or she stood, implying there was nothing more to say.

These kinds of questions and statements were not limited to doorstep contacts. The pro-lifers were the only group that as spectators would press their issue on candidates in parades. When I marched in parades, I would always greet and shake hands with people in the crowd. Most spectators will either shake your hand, whatever their political views, or keep their distance. The pro-lifers, however, would invite me to approach them, then ask, "Are you pro-life?" and conspicuously refuse to shake my hand when I did not give the one-word answer they wanted. They confronted in the same way our parade volunteers as they handed out stickers with my name. One volunteer told me he always replied, "Everyone is pro-life."

Many committed pro-lifers made their views as public as possible by featuring large posters by their front door. The most common such poster announced in huge letters, "Thank God for Life." I usually noted these as "TGFL" in my door-knocking notes. There were one or two other posters of the same size with equivalent messages. One said "Choose Life!" Another featured a quote by Pope John Paul II on the sanctity of life. Cars in the driveway sometimes featured bumper stickers such as: "Half of the people who enter an abortion clinic don't come out alive."

Because the committed pro-lifers often publicly marked their residences, it would have been easy enough for me to skip those houses in my door knocking, as many people advised me to do. My chance of getting a vote out of a TGFL household was very slim. Nevertheless, I went to the door (though I felt a certain relief if no one was home). There were several reasons why I persisted in what looks like a waste of time. Most importantly, I did not want the pro-lifers to believe I was afraid of them. If I had door-knocked a neighborhood and conspicuously avoided approaching TGFL-marked households, everyone in the neighborhood would soon know it, and I would look like I had something to hide. This would simply reinforce the perception of the pro-life movement as a power to be afraid of, which is exactly what I wanted to challenge. Furthermore, my abortion statement invited dialogue, and that invitation would be demonstrably hollow if I preemptively cut off dialogue before it began. And if I were to win the election, I would have certain obligations toward those who voted against me because of abortion, such as providing constituent service and a willingness to work together on other issues. To skip conspicuously the houses of pro-lifers would imply that I was as single-issue as they were, and that if I were elected they could never approach me about anything. I definitely did not want to send such a message.

Quantifying the Pressure

In preparing to write this chapter I decided to count how frequently someone pressed me on the abortion issue in the course of my door knocking. In a good-sized sample of 2,139 contacts, I recorded 113 people, or 5.28 percent, who identified themselves as pro-life, either verbally or through a conspicuous poster or sign. This compares with 12 people, or .56 percent, who identified themselves as pro-choice. I want to emphasize that these self-identifications were always at the contact's initiative: I did not mention the issue in my standard literature piece, and I never initiated conversations on the subject.

There were geographical variations in this sample. Contacts were, for example, far more likely to self-identify as pro-life in St. Stephen or Albany than they were in Sartell or St. Joseph. During the campaign I was keenly aware of these regional differences without having to do a count.

In my original door-knocking notes I distinguished between "pro-life absolutist" and "pro-life but not absolutist." This particular distinction was from my perspective very important. A pro-life absolutist meant someone for whom opposition to abortion determined their vote; all other issues were secondary. A pro-life nonabsolutist meant someone opposed to abortion but who weighed that among other issues in deciding how to vote. There was a lot of guesswork in assigning people to "absolutist" and "nonabsolutist" categories, and I know I made some misjudgments.

These numbers are not intended as a sample of public opinion on abortion in the district. That requires regular social-scientific surveys of a kind I was in no position to conduct. What my raw count attempts to measure, instead, is the *degree of pressure* the pro-life movement was able to place upon legislative candidates day in, day out over the course of a long campaign. When someone flat out refused to support me without explanation or refused to talk to me at all, this could happen for any number of reasons, and it did not send any specific message. When someone told me they would not support me unless I was pro-life, it sent a message.

The relatively low number of self-identified pro-lifers in my sample (about one in nineteen contacts) surprised me at first. During the campaign it felt more like one in five, and that is what I might have guessed if I had not done the count. But the actual degree of pressure was higher than this initial count would suggest. One reason is that only about a third of my doorstep contacts were willing to express an opinion on any political issue at all. If we count only those contacts who expressed definite opinions on some political issue, the proportion of committed pro-lifers goes up to about one in every six or seven, which is much closer to my remembered experience. It is still nowhere close to a majority of contacts, but abortion probably came up more than any other single issue, almost always from a pro-life perspective. And it was pressed on me with an intensity that was unmatched by any other issues by individuals who were more likely to vote than the average citizen.

One will notice that the number of self-identifying pro-life contacts in my sample is about ten times the number of self-identifying pro-choice contacts. Steve Frank's poll numbers indicated a much closer division of opinion on this issue in Stearns County. So did respondents' answers to the abortion question on the UDF phone surveys we completed in District 14A ("Are you mainly pro-life? Mainly pro-choice? Somewhere in between?"). There may be any number of reasons why pro-choice voters self-identified so much more rarely. Some might have been intimidated into silence; some might have considered it pointless given the history of legislative candidates in both parties bowing to the MCCL; some might have been less inclined than their pro-life counterparts (at least in this district) to vote on the basis of a single issue, so that I recorded them as talking to me about other issues. But whatever the reason, this ten-to-one ratio tends to reinforce candidates' judgment in districts like mine that pro-lifers have to be listened to and pro-choicers do not.

112 ◄ Abortive Dialogue

Absolutist or Not?

The majority of my doorstep contacts with committed pro-lifers were brief because from their perspective there was nothing to say except "yes" or "no," and no other issues were worth discussing. In my door-knocking notes I have dozens of entries that simply read, "pro-life absolute," "*very* pro-life," "pro-life and nasty," or "pro-life — 'murder, murder.'"

In a few cases I clearly let the conversation continue too long instead of moving on to other voters. To one pro-life absolutist I argued that outlawing all abortions would simply produce millions of illegal abortions and women and teenage girls would die. In reply he insisted, contrary to fact, that legal abortions were just as dangerous as illegal ones. It is pointless to debate when there are no shared premises whatsoever.

At the St. Anna parish festival I talked for quite a while with a pro-lifer who, in reply to my willingness to allow legal abortions in the first trimester, dangled in front of my eyes an imitation fetus made of plastic, about the size of a dashboard ornament. He apparently carried this around for use in exactly such arguments. "How can you tell me this isn't a child?" he demanded. Here too I probably let the conversation go on too long.

But there were many cases where I believe I was right to continue the conversation. When I marked someone as "pro-life but not absolutist," it was usually because they were willing to talk seriously about issues besides abortion, and/or because they were willing to take seriously my own position on abortion rather than immediately dismissing it. No one said to me precisely, "I'm pro-life but not absolutist." Those categories were my own guesswork. What led me to place someone in the not-absolutist category was their signaling through words or body language that the conversation was not over when I did not give them a simple answer on abortion. I know I made misjudgments in lots of cases, but if everyone in the district who considered abortion an evil had voted against me, the election would not have been close.

The contacts I marked as "not absolutist" made up fewer than half of the cases where someone brought up abortion. But they are worth reporting because I believe they were more genuinely representative of opinion in the district than were the absolutists. Pro-life absolutists turned up more frequently in my door-knocking notes because they were far more likely to bring up the issue immediately and exclusively. Where people I classified as pro-life nonabsolutists turn up in my notes, I typically recorded them also talking to me about other issues. Here are some examples.

"Teaches at Catholic school, favors vouchers, liked my abortion statement."

"Asked about abortion, didn't seem absolutist, seemed interested in flier" (which meant the conversation wasn't already over).

"Pro-life but seemed satisfied with my approach."

"Pro-life, pro-voucher, but thought I had good points."

"Very pro-life but also favors contraception. Didn't seem absolutist." (In rural Stearns County to favor contraception marks someone out as an independent thinker.)

"Talked about union things. Abortion issue not determining."

"Asked about abortion (seemed satisfied). Worried about Minnesota water being piped down to Nevada." (This latter issue came up more than once during the campaign.)

"Worried about lake issues." (This was by Watab Lake in Pleasant Acres.) "Water got better after St. Joe went on sewage system. Asked about abortion—send him full statement."

Voters who considered abortion wrong but spent time talking to me about other issues were especially promising prospects. This suggested that my position on other issues attracted them enough to outweigh the disagreement over abortion. Many of the pro-life absolutists, in contrast, disagreed with me on so many other issues that I would never have gotten their vote anyway.

There was at least one case where I believe a couple displaying a "Thank God for Life" poster might have seriously considered voting for me. She was a chemical dependency counselor in the public schools; he worked in the mental health unit at a nearby hospital and also had a degree in gerontology. (We swapped stories about the Albany nursing home administrator whom I describe in chapter 2.) Health care was their big issue. The TGFL poster was there by the door the whole time, but they never raised the issue with me. This could have meant their position was so clear that it did not need to be stated. Alternatively, it could have meant they took my candidacy seriously and did not want to publicly mark themselves as single-issue voters. There is no way I can know for sure. I am certain, however, that this doorstep conversation was not a waste of my time or of theirs.

The Other Side

Those voters who told me they were pro-choice always did so in the course of conversations about more than one issue. The following example is typical. In August when I was door-knocking in Avon Township, where the pro-life movement was well-organized, I met a union plumber whose wife ran a small business. We talked for a while about workers' compensation reform, an issue he could view from one side as a union man and from another side as co-owner of a business. He identified himself as pro-choice. But I also marked that he "wanted to talk about every category in my flier."

In Sartell one June afternoon I talked over a backyard fence with two women, neighbors or friends. One was a nurse, and we spoke about health care issues. The two women had clearly talked to one another about the abortion issue in the past because one of them said to me, "Both of us are pro-choice." This led me to wonder whether pro-choice voters in the district were more likely to talk about the issue among themselves than to raise it with local legislative candidates.

In St. Joseph in August I spoke with one pro-choice person whose remarks were as forceful as anything expressed to me by the other side. She taught at Rocori High School in Cold Spring, where pro-life activism is stronger than in St. Joseph. "I'm tired of having pro-life forced down my throat," she said.

I suspect that most of my doorstep conversations with pro-choice voters occurred in cases where they did not self-identify, and as a result my notes classify them according to their views on some other issue. But if they were reluctant to initiate discussions of the issue, some of them did not hesitate to respond to the other side when they believed it necessary. At our October 6 debate in St. Joseph, both candidates were asked their views on abortion, and Dehler responded that "life begins at conception, and choice ends at conception." Soon afterward he was pressed with a hostile follow-up question from a member of the audience: "Just to clarify, are you saying that in cases of rape, incest, or the life of the mother, you would not support abortion as a choice?" He made clear that he would outlaw abortion even in cases of rape or incest. There was another equally skeptical follow-up question to which he replied, "I don't believe that anybody who lets their child come to full term will not love it." I do not think he won himself much support in the room with that answer. I suspect the false appearance of a pro-life consensus in the district left him unprepared for this kind of questioning. By this time in the campaign I was used to being the target of hostile abortion questions, and it was refreshing for once to see the tables turned.

Sending and Receiving Letters

The abortion controversy drove me to write more letters than any other issue during the campaign. I sent letters to the executive directors of activist organizations on both sides of the issue. I also wrote to many individual voters who had raised the issue with me in conversation, and a few wrote to me on their own initiative.

When I returned my MCCL questionnaire on July 21, I enclosed a letter addressed to Jackie Schwietz, the organization's executive director. I said I wanted to explain my position on abortion in greater detail than was possible in the "yes"/"no" format of their questionnaire. I described the restrictions I was willing to accept and included a copy of my abortion statement. I emphasized in the letter that "I believe that abortion is an evil to be remedied, not a morally neutral act. . . . But I believe there is room for honest disagreement as to the methods by which we as a society work to remedy the evil." I argued that an absolute prohibition "would do nothing whatsoever to solve the social problems that lead to abortion in the first place, and would produce disobedience and disrespect for law on a massive scale." I stressed prevention and said I wanted to encourage people on both sides of this debate "to seek some practical common ground" to that purpose. I made clear that I was not seeking the MCCL's endorsement, nor was I seeking endorsement or funds from organizations on the other side of the issue. Instead, I was writing because I wanted to keep lines of communication open and promised that "I would be willing to work with you in those areas where we agree." I also wanted to "eliminate any grounds for inaccurate characterization of my position on this issue." I said I would be willing to meet with representatives of the organization to further clarify my position if necessary.

I received no reply. I do not know whether my letter was thrown away or kept as ammunition.

At the same time I was enclosing explanatory letters along with my answers to questionnaires from pro-choice organizations: the Minnesota Women's Political Caucus, the Abortion Rights Council of Minnesota, and Planned Parenthood. Because my position on abortion was more restrictive than theirs, I was worried they would see no essential difference between my opponent and me and would discourage pro-choice voters from supporting either candidate. The political strongholds of pro-choice organizations lay in the Twin Cities and its suburbs, and I feared they would have little understanding of the political circumstances of my district.

In my letter to the Minnesota Women's Political Caucus I described my position on abortion, enclosed my statement, and pointed out that "no one in either party has ever run for office in this district except on a 100 percent anti-abortion platform. The MCCL is by far the strongest political force in the area, and I will be their prime target in this fall's election." I mentioned that my opponent favored a ban on abortion under any circumstances. I added that though I favored greater restrictions on late-term abortions, I was "absolutely opposed to all 'gag rules' and to any limitations on the use of Medicaid funds for abortions: whatever rules we make must apply equally to rich and poor." (I told the MCCL the same thing in their questionnaire.) Again I emphasized prevention, which I believed "can serve as the basis for some limited common efforts between people on opposite sides of the abortion debate." I emphasized that I was not seeking PAC funds (which would have been politically suicidal in my district), but I hoped they would communicate to their supporters that I was the better of the two candidates. I said I was willing to meet to discuss the matter further. I sent similar letters to the Abortion Rights Council and Planned Parenthood.

I never received any replies to these letters either. Whatever sympathy they may have had for my situation, I suspect that electing me was not a priority. They never expected legislators from rural Stearns County to support their agenda anyway.

This attempt to stay in communication with both sides and encourage common efforts at prevention must strike many readers as especially quixotic. But it is the political stances that have become entrenched around this issue, not the fact of abortion itself, that make common ground appear impossible. Activists on both sides of this issue have a political interest in eliminating the possibility of any middle ground, and in that respect I was challenging them both. I was writing these letters principally to clarify my own thinking and preserve my independence of action on abortion should I be elected.

I got more response from individual voters on this issue than I did from organizations. I have described above how I met many voters in the district who were opposed to abortion but considered my approach reasonable. I also heard from several who listened to me carefully but remained unconvinced. The story about the man from Holdingford with which I opened this chapter is one example. He called me on the phone because he wanted to hear my side of it before deciding whether to withdraw his support.

Early in the campaign I received a letter from a woman whom I had met at a Morrison County event. She and her husband were longtime Democrats but alienated from the party because of the abortion issue. She said she was sorry she could not support my campaign. "There is nothing more important than life. You say there are a lot of other important issues. Yes, there are, but without life, nothing matters because you don't exist. . . . You and I could get along just fine if it wasn't for the Abortion issue."

In late October I received a letter from a Royalton woman who reported that she had met me, looked over my campaign materials, and listened to me on the radio. She went on to complain, "You are trying to ride the middle of the fence, and that just doesn't work. The Bible even says, 'Be either hot or cold, not lukewarm, or I will spit you out of my mouth.' So can't you see that if you are on the side of saving lives, you must be totally there. Not 'We can cut back on abortions.' Also teaching at a Catholic college, you have a lot of influence on people, especially Catholics. You have a great privilege and *responsibility* to uplift their faith by standing up totally for life."

I had invited dialogue, and I was getting it. At least these individuals listened to what I was saying, took the time to write or call, did not misrepresent my position, and did not accuse me of being evil. This was better than a three-word question or accusation followed by a closed door. In this community civil discourse among people who disagreed about abortion was an accomplishment.

Abortion on the Radio

By mid-October our enormous early anxieties about the abortion controversy had diminished. The abortion issue was always present, but it did not derail my campaign. Our internal surveys indicated the race was very close despite the MCCL's staunch opposition to me. We believed the abortion issue had been successfully contained and planned to use the final weeks campaigning on themes that played to my strengths.

But events took a different turn. What triggered the final, strange series of campaign actions and reactions was my October 20 appearance as a morning talk show guest on KASM radio in Albany.

These hour-long shows follow a standard format. The show host interviews a guest during the first part of the show, followed by call-in questions from listeners. When a candidate for office appears on the show, supporters usually line up to call in softball questions, while opponents try to pack the show with hostile questions. In this instance, however, we dropped the ball and had not arranged any callers. The opposition had.

In the first part of the show the host, Cliff Mitchell, asked whether voters in the district "warmed up" to me as a college professor and recent transplant to a community that, as he put it, was "very German, *Katolisch,* and clannish." He had me talk about the projected state budget deficit, education, and agriculture and wanted to know why everyone we sent to St. Paul seemed to lose their common sense. There was a short break featuring a very detailed farm report and announcements of local auctions. Then we went to the phone lines. Most of the questions or comments concerned abortion.

The first caller was a man who said he wanted to know my views on abortion and gun control. His tone suggested he did not support me, but the questions were fair, and I had expected them. I treated gun control briefly, saying I would leave in place Minnesota's current restrictions but impose no new ones. Then I described my position on abortion and the reasoning behind it in some detail: that abortion was an evil and our goal should be to reduce its numbers, that I would be as happy as anyone to see it disappear, but the absolute prohibition favored by my opponent was unenforceable — unless we wanted to declare a "war on abortion" like the war on drugs and tie up our police, courts, and jails with women who had illegal abortions. I said that many women might be freely persuaded not to have an abortion if they were genuinely informed of all options and had the social supports they needed. I lamented that the political positions on this issue had become like two opposing armies, when no one really wants abortion to occur. I closed by saying, "It seems to me if we put half the amount of time and energy and political will into prevention and persuasion and changing the conditions that lead to abortion in the first place, we would have far fewer of them than we do today."

The next caller, after a long preface praising my opponent's experience and judgment, continued with the abortion issue. "Jim, you call it an evil. How can you allow something that you call an evil? . . . If something is evil, should it not be disallowed by statute? We know it's going to occur anyway, but to give the sanction of law to an evil doesn't seem to me to be a responsible moral choice." The man was clearly thoughtful and had listened carefully to my response to the previous caller.

In my reply I first emphasized that I would not allow abortions in later stages of pregnancy where a prohibition is more readily enforceable. But an absolute prohibition on all abortions "would be massively disobeyed and lead to disrespect for law. I think that's one of the differences between a moral position, where one can state things in terms of absolutes, and a law. Morally you can say that abortion is an evil and convince a person who would otherwise have one not to do it." But if as a legislator I did not think such a law was enforceable, and that it would lead to bad consequences — "for instance, women dying of illegal abortions — that's a pro-life issue for me too" — then I could not support that kind of law. "So not every evil can be corrected simply by passing laws against it. It's the same with gun control. I think in a lot of ways the idea of stopping murder by taking away guns is a little bit similar to the idea that you will stop abortion by banning all abortions."

With the gun control analogy I was trying to make an argument that everyone in a politically conservative community would understand. If I had simply said, "Every woman has a right to her own reproductive freedom," it would have fallen on deaf ears.

The next caller, a woman, would not let the abortion issue go and would not address me directly. "I would like to know how he thinks it will be OK for a woman to abort her baby at twelve weeks, when life begins with conception. Also I understand he's a teacher. If he would be one of those aborted, he wouldn't be a teacher today. To me abortion is murder. I thank you, I'd like his comments."

This was a much more hostile call, but months of door knocking had prepared me for it. I replied, "Well, I've already said a couple of times about the abortion issue that I'm not going to pass a law that I can't enforce. As far as where life begins, I don't know. I'm a candidate for office. All I know is that people have very great disagreements about this, and I as a candidate for office don't know how to force people who have very different religious beliefs to believe differently than they do. What I can do, as I said before, is support programs that will reduce the number of abortions that occur. That kind of thing is in my power. People's religious beliefs are not." Many people in the district had never been asked to distinguish between religious beliefs and laws, and I was pressing them to do so.

The next question, hostile but vague, asked me whether I favored free enterprise or socialism. There was a question from a supporter of private-school vouchers, and one softball question about health care from one of my supporters who somehow squeezed past the pro-lifers tying up the phone lines.

Then we got a call from a woman whose remarks made the whole long campaign seem worthwhile. She had a definite Stearns County accent and was not one of my campaign volunteers or anyone I knew. "Good morning. I have a comment for the representative rather than a question. I'm with him, and I understand where he's coming from on the abortion issue. Even though everybody gives him heck about it." I replied, "Thank you very much."

This suggested to me that my stance on abortion was resonating with ordinary voters in the district. The caller was not a political insider (referring to me as "the representative" proved that), and her call had not been arranged by either campaign. She had simply been listening to the show, thought what I said about abortion was reasonable, and was willing to side with me in spite of the "heck" anyone gets in this community for voicing a dissenting opinion.

I believed that I had stood up well under more than a half hour of pro-life pressure over the airwaves. Cliff Mitchell was hard to read, but I think he respected my performance whatever his views on the issue itself. That day I had worn some kind of light-colored turtleneck under a dark sweater. After the show as I was saying goodbye, Cliff said, "Jim, just a word of advice. You might want to get rid of the turtleneck. You don't want anyone confusing you with a priest."

Pia had listened to the broadcast and taped it. "I was so proud of you," she said. The pro-lifers had put intense public pressure on me, and unlike any local candidate they had encountered before, I had stood up to them. The open debate about abortion that had just taken place over the local airwaves was exactly what had always been lacking in this community; I considered it a sign of political health. Whatever ultimately happened on election day, I believed I had accomplished something important.

However, not everyone who heard the broadcast considered it a healthy exchange. A number of people were extremely alarmed and decided something had to be done. If I would not bend under the pressure, they could find someone who would.

An Ugly Turn of Events

On the evening of the same day, October 20, that I appeared on KASM radio and defended my stance on abortion, I was in my campaign office along with a group of volunteers preparing a mass mailing: a letter of endorsement Rep. Jeff Bertram had written on my behalf, to be sent to two thousand households currently in his district (16B in the pre-1992 numbering) that had been moved to 14A when redistricting changed the boundaries. This redistricted zone included Albany, Albany Township, Krain Township, and several towns and townships in Morrison County. For these two thousand households, Jeff Bertram, not Bernie Omann, was the incumbent, so a letter of endorsement would be especially helpful to my campaign.

In the middle of our stuffing and stamping envelopes, I got a phone call from Jeff Bertram. He asked, "Have you sent out that letter?" I said not yet. He then announced, "That letter is not going out." He repeated it several times for emphasis. He had withdrawn his letter of endorsement.

He told me he had received at least fifty phone calls that day, including one from his own parish priest, demanding that he not publicly endorse me. "My own parish priest," he repeated. He told me my appearance on KASM radio that morning had triggered an organized campaign by the MCCL to pressure him to withdraw the letter. Apparently an officer of the local Republican Party, whom Jeff named, had discovered or guessed that he might write me a letter of endorsement. This individual (according to Jeff's account) had contacted Jackie Schwietz, executive director of the MCCL, who passed it along to the local MCCL chapter, which within a few hours had mobilized this intense pressure campaign.

Jeff confessed that he had made matters worse by lying and claiming no such letter existed. So if I were to send out the letter, he would not only be outraging abortion opponents but would be caught in a lie.

Jeff Bertram literally did not have an opponent in 1992—not even a name on the ballot. None of this pressure could have caused him to lose his seat in this year's election. One might suppose that he would simply dismiss this as a last-minute political stunt by a local Republican Party who had failed to field its own candidate in Jeff's district. But that would be overlooking the dominant political position of the MCCL in rural Stearns County. It was the MCCL—stronger than any party in the district—that was turning on the heat. Both Jeff and Joe Bertram had used the MCCL as a key political base throughout their political careers. The MCCL had made him, and they could unmake him, if not immediately, then the next time around.

Jeff Bertram had known my position on abortion from the beginning of the campaign. He said he would support me as long as it was clear to everyone that he himself was 100 percent pro-life. For most of the campaign he had supported me behind the scenes but shied away from a public endorsement. In the letter itself—a well-written letter, I might add—he covered himself on the abortion issue by saying, "I will admit that I don't agree with Jim on every issue, and there is certainly no reason why I should, but I think he is an excellent choice for the area." He praised my energetic effort "to go door-to-door and develop that one-on-one relationship with the people he will represent in the State Legislature." By the time he finally wrote the public letter of endorsement, I assumed he had calculated his political risk on the abortion issue and judged it acceptable. He had obviously miscalculated.

The timing of the MCCL pressure campaign also surprised me. The statewide organization and its local members had known my position on abortion for months. My questionnaire responses had been reported a while ago in their member newsletter, and I had communicated my views in conversation to dozens of individual activists. What I had said in my October 20 radio appearance was no different than what I had been saying all along.

It was the *public* defense of my views over the radio in response to pro-life pressure that stirred up the hornets. It was one thing for my views to be expressed in individual conversations and letters. It was another thing to voice them unapologetically over the radio, in a way that no one had ever experienced before in this community. What made it worse was that a listener had called in to say she agreed with me. This made me a greater threat than before and triggered the sudden and highly effective pressure campaign on Jeff.

In the course of my phone conversation with Jeff, events then became even stranger and uglier. He showed a side of his character I had never seen before. Here I want to quote the report of this phone conversation from my own sworn testimony to the Minnesota House Ethics Committee on March 15, 1996, when Jeff Bertram was being investigated for a broad pattern of alleged intimidation and slander. "Jeff Bertram then told me he was going to 'get back at ——' by circulating rumors that —— had molested boys at a Boy Scout camp. He said this as though I too would want to get revenge on ——, which was strange because all —— had done was leak the existence of a letter I was just about to send to two thousand households. I said, 'Jeff, don't do that. I don't want my name dragged into something like that.' I told him I would not send out the letter without his permission, but he couldn't spread those rumors. Jeff Bertram then promised me he wouldn't do it."

I am certain that what Jeff alleged about this Republican activist was a complete fabrication for purposes of political retaliation. Since that time I have seen him make equally groundless accusations against others (which are also described in my March 15, 1996, testimony).

The slander threat raised issues too large and distracting for me to focus on at the moment. (That part of the story will resume in chapter 6.) My immediate problem was that we had made a huge investment of money and volunteer time preparing a mailing that I had now promised Jeff I would not send out without his permission. Every campaign volunteer in the room at the time agreed with Pia that I should simply send out the letter: we had it in our hands, and there was nothing Jeff could do to stop us. (When I told Jim Graeve I was writing this memoir, the first thing he said was, "Don't forget the part about how you would have been elected if you'd sent out Jeff Bertram's letter.") I called Dee Long, the speaker of the House, who tried unsuccessfully to get Jeff to change his mind. She then likewise advised me simply to send out the letter.

There were three reasons I declined to follow this unanimous advice. Jeff's panicked state of mind during the phone conversation made me fear that if I sent out the letter, he would follow it with an equally public retraction (there was time enough before the election for him to do this) or even claim that I had forged the letter. None of this would have made him look good, but a public controversy would not have helped my campaign either. Second, I had promised Jeff I would not send it without his permission, and I felt obligated to honor that promise. Finally, I feared that if I sent out the letter, he would follow through on the slander campaign in a way that would somehow implicate me. None of the campaign volunteers urging me to send the letter had witnessed this poisonous side of the evening's events in the way that I had. By this point I honestly did not want the endorsement of Jeff Bertram as I was now seeing him.

What made this worse was that I had been on good terms with Jeff through most of the campaign, despite disagreements on abortion and fund-raising strategy. I had said nice things about him on that morning's radio broadcast (which probably made his situation worse). I had been genuinely looking forward to working with him as a legislative colleague and friend. Now I was definitely on my own in what had become an increasingly hostile political environment.

The Zylla Ad

After the Jeff Bertram episode we were sure we would be hit directly on the abortion issue sometime before election day, but we did not know what form it would take. We waited anxiously and prepared ourselves to respond.

By the late stages of the campaign, it had become very difficult, at least from my perspective, to distinguish between the Steve Dehler legislative campaign and the election-related activities of the MCCL. The successful pressure on Jeff Bertram to withdraw his letter could only have worked as an MCCL initiative. As a Democratic legislator he would not have withdrawn the letter under pressure from the Dehler Volunteer Committee.

About a week before the election, the Dehler campaign sent out a mass mailing that was focused entirely on abortion. It was nearly indistinguishable in content from the independent-expenditure mailings the MCCL was simultaneously doing in the district (also targeting me). Dehler's mailing led with the MCCL's billboard slogan, "Abortion: the Leading Cause of Death in Minnesota," and featured a photo of a six-month-old baby beside a caption that read, "She Needs Your Vote Tuesday, Nov. 3." There was also a

graphic photo of a fetus. The text of the mailing compared Dehler's absolute opposition to abortion with my responses to the MCCL questionnaire
(e.g., that I would not vote to outlaw RU-486) and quoted me from a news
story saying, "Prohibition of abortion won't solve any problems."

The presentation of my position was one-sided but not inaccurate,
and we were not especially alarmed by its content. More troublesome
was the timing and volume of the mailing. We decided we would need
to do another large mailing ourselves to respond on abortion and several
other last-minute issues. But then we were hit with something completely
unexpected.

On the evening of Friday, October 30, the last weekend before the election, I was in my campaign office calling people who had promised they
would vote for me, to reconfirm their support and remind them to vote
on Tuesday. One woman reassured me she still supported me and added,
"And I think that radio ad with the priest is just awful." This was how I
found out about the Zylla ad.

Father Paul Zylla was well-known in Stearns County. He was the former Pro-Life Director of the St. Cloud Diocese, a position he had created
in 1970 and in which he had served for two decades. To the pro-lifers in
the community he was a pioneer and key leader. His many critics sometimes referred to him as "God-Zylla." (I have it on Bob Spaeth's authority
that Zylla had threatened Hubert Humphrey with eternal damnation.) By
1992 he was no longer Pro-Life Director for the diocese but was still active in pro-life activities and, we had now discovered, in local legislative
campaigns.

Beginning on Friday, October 30, the Dehler campaign began saturat-
ing radio stations in and around the district with the following one-minute
political ad. It is Zylla's voice throughout the ad except for the brief tag
line at the end.

"I am Father Paul Zylla of Royalton. In House District 14A Steve
Dehler is a pro-life candidate whose views coincide with the long-
standing and solid pro-life values of this area.

"His opponent, Jim Read, emphasized that he is not pro-choice, but clearly there is a vocabulary problem here. Jim Read would outlaw abortion only after the twelfth week of pregnancy; he must know that over 90 percent of all abortions take place in the first twelve weeks, but he would not object. Jim Read is certainly pro-abortion, he stands for the pro-abortion status quo. He is someone Planned Parenthood considers pro-choice.

"We are shocked at his lack of comprehension of the issue and his obvious vocabulary problem, despite his position as a college teacher.

"The man who fits the ideals of pro-life 14A is Steve Dehler."

[Tag line in Dehler's voice]: "Paid for by the Dehler Volunteer Committee."

The surprising thing here is not the text of the ad itself, but that a Catholic priest would appear in a paid political advertisement. Because of his former position as spokesman for the St. Cloud Diocese, many listeners may have missed the very quick tag line and assumed incorrectly that Zylla was speaking officially for the diocese in this ad. This confusion may have been intended.

Even in Stearns County it was unusual to use religion so directly for political purposes. The Catholic Church makes clear its opposition to abortion, but as an institution it stops short of officially endorsing candidates in paid political advertisements. I doubt that the Dehler campaign — or rather the MCCL contingent leading that campaign — would have run an ad like this unless they suspected the election was close and that my moderate position on abortion was resonating with a number of voters in the district.

Several elements of the ad deserve notice. The phrase about the "long-standing strong and solid pro-life values of this area" was intended to reinforce the view that this community was completely united in seeking to outlaw all abortions and that anyone who voiced a different view displayed a "lack of comprehension" and was not really a member of the community. The notion that one might consider abortion bad but oppose it through other measures than coercive laws was excluded from the outset:

I was obviously "pro-abortion." The ad also implied that I should not be allowed to teach at a Catholic college. There were some gratuitous insults about my "vocabulary problem" thrown in for good measure.

After the election Dehler himself admitted to the *St. Joseph Newsleader* (November 20) that he had approved the Zylla ad "but did not design it and had not even heard the broadcast." This further suggests that in the final days his campaign had in effect become a vehicle for the MCCL.

We knew we had to respond to the Zylla ad. Bob Spaeth (a lifelong Catholic) believed I had a moral obligation to respond to this abuse of religious authority for political purposes. He argued that I could pick up votes from local Catholics who had been subjected to this kind of religious manipulation for years from Zylla and others and were sick of it.

We had only a day to script, record, hand-deliver, and pay for the following one-minute radio ad. Pia had to deliver it in the middle of a snowstorm to three widely dispersed radio stations, in St. Cloud, Albany, and Little Falls. The voice was my own except for the tag line. We had to record it several times because Pia thought I did not sound outraged enough on the first take.

"This is Jim Read, candidate for state representative in District 14A. My opponent, Steve Dehler, is currently broadcasting a paid political ad in which a Catholic priest from the district, Father Paul Zylla of Royalton, attacks me by name, falsely claims that I am pro-abortion, and falsely asserts that Planned Parenthood is in some way connected with my campaign.

"I am outraged that my opponent is willing to use religion for his political gain. I am also dismayed that a priest would display such lack of judgment as to speak on behalf of a candidate in a paid political advertisement.

"This is nothing less than an attempt to use religious authority to manipulate Catholic voters into voting for my opponent. I resent this kind of politics of intimidation, and I won't be intimidated. I will continue my battle to be elected state representative in District 14A."

[Tag line in Pia's voice]: "Paid for by Jim Read Campaign Committee."

I clearly sound embattled in this ad, and that is the way we felt. My response to pro-life callers on the radio had been followed in close succession by Jeff Bertram's withdrawn letter, the mass mailing naming me as an enemy of babies and fetuses, and the Zylla ad, all right before the election. The reader may recall that anxieties about abortion politics had almost prevented me from running at all. What happened in the last two weeks of the campaign proved that our early anxieties were well-founded. But it also meant we were mentally prepared for this kind of thing. We knew all along what we were getting into.

Our purpose in the response ad was to turn the attack around. Even voters very opposed to abortion might resent a priest telling them how to vote, and a candidate using a priest for this purpose.

At the same time that we prepared our response ad, we were trying energetically to convince the press that a paid political ad with a priest telling people how to vote was a newsworthy story. I called the *St. Cloud Times,* the *Minneapolis Star-Tribune,* and the *St. Paul Pioneer Press,* encouraging them to look into the story. I was never able to interest anyone at these newspapers. I was asked, "Are you claiming that there's any violation of law involved?" I replied that as far as I knew a priest appearing in a paid political ad did not violate any law — it was just extremely inappropriate. (If Zylla had pretended to speak officially for the diocese in endorsing a candidate for office, it would have violated the church's tax-exempt status, but the ad did not literally cross this line.) "But out in Stearns County, does anyone think it's inappropriate?" one of the editors asked, here reinforcing the old stereotype. I did persuade D. J. Leary, coeditor of *Politics in Minnesota,* to mention the Zylla ad in his newsletter, and the *St. Joseph Newsleader* took it seriously but did not go to press until after the election.

The press's lack of interest in the story strongly contrasts with the intense attention given in the closing days of the 1990 U.S. Senate campaign to incumbent Rudy Boschwitz's letter to some members of the Minnesota Jewish community attacking his challenger Paul Wellstone for not properly following the Jewish faith.[1] The public backlash from that ill-considered letter helped Wellstone win the election. Boschwitz's letter did not violate any law either, yet the press considered it a newsworthy story. A U.S. Senate campaign was obviously higher profile than my state legislative campaign. But I believe another reason for the differing response was that the Boschwitz letter came as a shock, whereas the Zylla ad was simply what outsiders expected of Stearns County.

Several years later I talked with a Republican activist and MCCL member who had had a hand in arranging the Zylla ad. He told me that "politically, you were running circles around Dehler. We needed to try something else." He said they had expected me to respond to the ad and judged that they would come out ahead on the exchange. Who actually came out ahead is anyone's guess. For at least a month before the election, long before the Zylla ad and the whole barrage of abortion-related political maneuvers, we had been predicting on the basis of our own surveys that this race would be decided by fewer than a hundred votes.

Perhaps Zylla's ad and my response changed no minds at all. That would be fine with me. The foundation of my campaign was direct conversations with voters at their doors. *That* was where I believe I changed minds. My exchange of radio ads with Father Zylla simply reproduced the "dialogue of the deaf" over abortion, which I had hoped all along to get beyond.

Democratizing the Decision

I did not run for office with the aim of converting anyone to my point of view on abortion. If elected, I did not intend to be a legislative leader on abortion, and I did not believe my own position on the issue would become law. I cared more about other issues, among them affordable health care, education, environmental protection, and the overall quality of our civic and political life. That was where I hoped to make my mark as a legislator.

As a candidate for office I never initiated conversations or arguments about abortion. Everything I said on the subject was in response to some individual or organization that made abortion a higher priority than I did.

I took the "middle ground" position I did because that had long been my actual view of the matter and I did not want to spend six months pretending to think differently. But I had always been willing to work with individuals and to support candidates whose views on abortion differed from my own.

I invited dialogue on abortion not because I valued abortion discussion for its own sake (I would have gladly avoided it), but because given my own views and the political history of the district, I had little choice. I could not avoid taking a position on the issue at all. I refused to say, "I am pro-life," when in our district this signified deference to a particular organization and ideology. I refused to say, "The Supreme Court has decided this matter once and for all," because in my district few people respected this kind of answer, and I did not believe it myself. To invite dialogue seemed my only remaining strategy.

This dialogue was stressful and drained time and energy away from issues I was more eager to discuss. But I do not believe the dialogue was pointless or a complete failure. If every exchange on the subject had been of the "murder, murder" variety, and if I had lost by a landslide, I would be more inclined to judge the effort a failure. But many of my abortion conversations, including some with voters who did not support me, were civil. And the election results suggest that I persuaded a number of voters either that my position on abortion was reasonable or that what I offered on other issues outweighed their disagreement with me on this one.

I do not recommend to everyone everywhere the particular position I took on abortion in an unsuccessful legislative campaign fifteen years ago. My statements on abortion resulted from my own personal views and the peculiar circumstances of the district. But I do believe that dialogue on this issue, abortive or otherwise, among people with very different religious and philosophical starting points is necessary and may become unavoidable in the coming decades.[2]

In 1992 it was unlikely the Supreme Court would reverse *Roe v. Wade* in the near future. Today the prospect is very real that the *Roe* precedent will be reversed or greatly weakened and much more discretion given to Congress and state legislatures to legislate on abortion — and not just at the margins. If this happens, decisions about abortion would be made to an increasing degree by the ordinary democratic process. Exchanges among voters, and between voters and candidates for elective office, would become relatively more important than courtroom exchanges in setting abortion policy.

The argument is sometimes made that to turn abortion over to the democratic process would be a full-scale disaster. The issue is too explosive, the argument goes. Better to keep it off the democratic agenda as much as possible and keep it in the courtroom. But there is little evidence that the judicialization of the abortion controversy has done anything to contain its explosive energies. It could be argued on the contrary that its effect has been to encourage extreme and irreconcilable rights claims, and extreme politics centered on those claims. Democratically elected legislative bodies are no more likely to resolve philosophical and theological disputes than courts are, but they might be able to achieve policy-level compromises that courts cannot. And at the very least democratizing the abortion issue would put to the test the claims made by each camp of opposing activists that the American people are really on their side.

When people say the abortion issue is too explosive to be left to the democratic process, I imagine they have in mind the kind of absolutist politics I faced in District 14A in 1992. But I lived through it. It was difficult, but it fell short of a worst-case scenario for democratic politics. Voters are not fools when it comes to abortion.

CHAPTER SIX

Countdown, Recount, and Retrospect

Last-minute stratagems would not win this election for me. Winning depended on the base I had built up over six months of door knocking. But we feared we could *lose* the election in the final days if voters whom I had persuaded to support me turned away because of some last-minute development or attack. A whole series of end-of-campaign crises threatened to erode the support I had worked so hard to build. Even if the number of voters swayed by last-minute communications was small, in a close election these last-minute shifts could be decisive.

The previous chapter has already described several final-weeks crises related to the abortion issue, including Jeff Bertram's withdrawn letter of endorsement under intense pro-life pressure (a timely windfall for my opponent) and my opponent's radio ad featuring a Catholic priest attacking me in an overwhelmingly Catholic district. On top of the abortion-related crises, I was the target of another painfully timed last-minute shot coming from a different direction: the National Rifle Association.

I had decided early in the campaign that I was not going to be a martyr to the gun issue. I knew I would have the pro-life groups against me, and I hoped to avoid a two-front battle. Moreover, any significantly restrictive position on guns would create consistency problems: having stressed the impossibility of enforcing a very restrictive antiabortion policy, I would be skewered if I suggested it was easier to enforce restrictive gun policies.

In Minnesota the political divisions over gun issues are geographical rather than partisan. In the Twin Cities metropolitan area, candidates can thumb their nose at the NRA without paying any political price. In outstate rural and small-town districts like mine, the conventional electoral wisdom in both parties was to give the NRA everything it wanted; it is not unusual to see Democratic and Republican candidates competing with one another for the NRA endorsement. (In the Seventh District congressional contest in 1992, for instance, both candidates received As from the NRA. In other local legislative races, Jeff Bertram received an A in his uncontested 14B race; Joe Bertram, incumbent District 14 state senator, received an A plus.)

I was unwilling to give the NRA *everything* it wanted. Instead, in my answers to their questionnaire I granted them everything my conscience would permit, and perhaps a bit more. The first question asked the candidate to take one of three possible general positions on Minnesota firearm laws: A, supporting new firearm restrictions; B, "current state laws are sufficient," and C, "current state laws should be reformed or repealed to benefit law-abiding gun owners and sportsmen." The NRA's favored answer was, of course, C; answering A would make oneself a declared enemy of the NRA. I marked the middle position, "current state laws are sufficient." My general position was to oppose any new firearms restrictions but to preserve and better enforce those state restrictions already on the books. In 1992 Minnesota had a five-day waiting period on handgun purchases (anticipating the national Brady Bill, which passed in 1993), and I did not propose to repeal this restriction. I also declined to support NRA-supported legislation that would make it impossible for police departments to deny a permit for concealed weapons to someone they considered high-risk. On most other matters I supported the NRA position (but would not promise to *sponsor* NRA-supported legislation). I opposed any legislation that would ban or register firearms. I supported adding a "right to keep and bear arms" to the Minnesota constitution.

In mid-October the NRA sent out its candidate ratings for Minnesota congressional and legislative candidates (prefaced by an admonition to "Use Your Firepower at the Ballot Box!"). My opponent, who gave them everything they wanted, received an A, which in the organization's terms meant "solidly pro-gun/pro-hunting, opposed to additional controls on firearms or legislation restricting hunting, and would vote for pro-gun reform legislation." I received a B plus, which in their terms meant "basically on our side, but might vote for some additional restrictions or might not support pro-gun/pro-hunting reform legislation." Unlike the MCCL mailing, which reported specifically how each candidate answered each question, the NRA mailing included only the grades. I was satisfied with my NRA grade. It was never my aim to win the NRA endorsement — I knew my opponent would get that — but merely to reassure individual NRA members that I was not the kind of dangerous antigun zealot that features so prominently in NRA election-year rhetoric. I believed my B-plus grade adequately communicated my position and that I had successfully neutralized the gun issue. But in the immortal words of Mae West, I was "suffering from a false delusion."

In the course of my campaign I had spoken several times with a man from Holding Township. He liked my stance on nearly everything, including abortion, but he was an NRA member, and he needed to be reassured that I was not anti–gun rights. In a long conversation at the Holdingford parish festival he questioned me at length on gun issues. I laid out my general position: that I would oppose any new restrictions but would keep in place the ones already on the books. I described how I had answered some of the specific questions on the NRA questionnaire. He pronounced himself satisfied with my position and said he would support me. A couple of weeks before the election he reconfirmed his support over the phone and said we could put up a large yard sign on his property, an excellent location on a well-traveled highway.

Less than a week before election day the national office of the NRA sent out a mass mailing to our district. This one was a bright orange card that boldly asserted that the enemies of firearms freedoms were on the march in this country and warned voters that if they wanted to preserve their constitutional rights, they should vote for Steve Dehler for state representative in District 14A. This time there was no grade and were no shadings of degree: it was all or nothing. The clear implication was that I was one of these dangerous "enemies" that had to be defeated.

I was surprised and shocked by this mailing and knew immediately it spelled trouble. In the mid-October mailing to NRA members my B-plus rating was buried on page 3 of a long list of candidates. This new, last-minute, district-specific mass mailing portrayed in black-and-white terms only one race and two candidates, with me targeted as the enemy. As it turns out, all my efforts at compromise and moderation on the NRA's issues counted for nothing. The text of the bright orange card would have been exactly the same if I had proposed confiscating every private weapon in the United States.

In retrospect I should not have been surprised. As a high-intensity political pressure group, the NRA wants to show that it can elect its endorsed candidates and defeat those candidates whom it has not endorsed. The whole charade of giving candidates objective-sounding "grades" on gun issues was subordinate to the real political objective, which was reward and punishment. My opponent had declared that he would take direction from the NRA. I had made no such declaration. It was as simple as that. The big orange card communicated nothing about my actual position on gun issues.

Unfortunately, I was unable to persuade the Holding Township man of this in the few days remaining before the election. As soon as I saw the mailing, I called him. He had already taken down the yard sign and said he would not vote for me. I reminded him that he had heard my position on gun issues in detail and found them acceptable. He replied, "I trust the organization on this." It became clear in the course of the phone conversation that he believed I had lied to him when I described my position on guns and imagined that the NRA had some new alarming information about my views that explained this last-minute attack. I assured him that I had said exactly the same thing to the NRA that I had said to him in person, and if he doubted me, I would drive over right away and show him my NRA questionnaire. But he was set against me. Still hoping to win back the man's support, and worried that others would follow his lead, I commissioned a supporter of mine who was active in the St. Joseph Rod and Gun Club to visit the Holding Township man with my questionnaire in hand.

My St. Joseph supporter told me after the election that the man admitted he had overreacted and that there was nothing in my answers to the NRA questionnaire that should have caused him to withdraw his support. He was less inflexible on gun issues than the organization to which he belonged. If the mailing had arrived two weeks before the election, I would have had time to persuade him and other voters with similar concerns that I was not the "enemy of firearm freedoms" featured in NRA campaign rhetoric. But of course the whole intention behind the NRA's last-minute mass mailing was to give its targets no opportunity to respond before election day.

Nevertheless, we decided to attempt a last-minute response on this and other matters. The only mailing we ever sent to every household in the district was produced, copied, and mailed within four days of the election.

All Night at Kinko's

We had all along anticipated the possibility of last-minute attacks and had reserved enough money in our campaign budget for some kind of response. But I had hoped it would be unnecessary and that we could spend our final days and dollars on positive messages central to my own campaign themes. We had never "gone negative" over the course of a long campaign. Now we decided to both respond and counterattack. My radio ad directly responding to my opponent's Father Zylla radio ad was described in the previous chapter. But we also decided on a "postal customer" mailing that, with luck, would get to every household in the district. The mailing covered three issues: abortion, "Firearms Freedoms," and the homestead tax credit. Neither the abortion nor gun issues had been mentioned in any of my previous campaign mailings or brochures. The homestead tax credit had been mentioned but never highlighted in previous campaign literature.

On abortion I said, "I believe abortion is an evil and must be reduced. The question is, should it be reduced through moral persuasion or through the coercive power of the criminal law?" I pointed out that my opponent "would use the force of the criminal law to outlaw abortion even in the case of rape and incest." I laid out the specifics of my position, said I welcomed dialogue on the issue, and gave my phone number.

The section on "Firearm Freedoms" was a response to the NRA's inflammatory independent mailing, not to anything my opponent had said about me. We said: "Jim Read thinks law-abiding gun owners should be left alone. That's why he received a B-plus rating from the National Rifle Association. Jim Read opposes any new gun restrictions and will preserve and promote your firearm freedoms in the legislature. And he'll work to preserve Minnesota's wildlife and natural beauty enjoyed by hunters and non-hunters alike." I was troubled then, and embarrassed now, that we made this sound as though the NRA was satisfied with me rather than targeting me. It would have felt better to point out the massive contradiction between their first giving me a B plus and then later denouncing me as an enemy of Second Amendment rights. But I did not feel politically strong enough at this stage of the campaign to launch a counterattack against the NRA.

The homestead tax credit was an issue we had been keeping in reserve since the October 6 candidate forum. At issue was a provision in the Minnesota property tax code that taxed single-family owner-occupied houses at a lower rate than second homes and rented houses. The program was understandably popular with families who owned one house and lived in it. Many low-income and elderly homeowners also benefited from another provision, the property tax refund program, which provided tax relief to homeowners whose property taxes were high relative to their incomes (and many voters did not clearly distinguish between the two programs). The homestead tax credit was criticized by some who thought it unnecessarily complicated the tax code or who believed commercial property was overtaxed and residential property undertaxed. Early on I had declared my support for preserving the homestead tax credit, but for most of the campaign it was simply one issue among many.

What changed its priority was a clumsy statement by my opponent in response to a question at the St. Joseph candidate forum on October 6. Our end-of-campaign mass mailing directly quoted our exchange on the issue. Steve Dehler: "My view would be to simplify it so that we can understand what is going on. If simplifying it means eliminating the homestead tax credit, that would be fine." Jim Read: "I think that if you simplified the homestead tax credit by eliminating it, you would simplify a lot of people out of their homes. Right now people are pretty much stretched to the limit with property taxes."

Immediately after that debate many of my campaign volunteers were urging me to take advantage of Dehler's blunder and directly attack him on the homestead tax credit. For three weeks I resisted this advice because I wanted to stay positive and avoid mentioning the opponent's name. But in the final days the combination of the Zylla radio ad and the NRA mailing had overcome my inhibitions about "going negative."

Our deadline to get this mailing out was noon the Friday before the election. Any later and it would not arrive before election day, though even if we met the deadline, there was no guarantee. Pia and I and one volunteer stayed up all night Thursday at Kinko's making ten thousand copies, as one machine after another overheated and jammed. Then we drove the mailings to the post office, where we bundled them by postal carrier routes and by zip codes and pleaded with postal workers to get them out as soon as possible. (A "postal customer" mailing is not addressed by name and has lower priority than other mailings.) We were doing all of this at the same time that we were recording and hand-delivering my radio ad response to the Zylla attack, on top of all the regular get-out-the-vote activities that our campaign was engaged in. The best we could hope for was that a critical mass of households would receive the mailing on the day before the election.

We do know now that many did arrive and at least some people read them. On the night before the election I was in the campaign office when the phone rang. An angry supporter of my opponent (who was caught off guard when I answered the phone myself) claimed that I had dishonestly misrepresented what Dehler had meant at the October 6 forum. The caller tried to explain at length how Dehler really only wanted to simplify the tax credit, not eliminate it. I pointed out that I had directly quoted Dehler's own words and added: "I don't care what he *meant*. I'm going by what he *said*."

Many voters are rightfully skeptical of any last-minute campaign mailing. We suspected most people would not read the piece (and I myself find it painful to reread now). But I wanted voters to see that I was at least responding to the attacks they had received in the mail and heard on the radio in the last week. I did not choose to act as though it was beneath me to respond. I wanted to look like a fighter.

The Times *Endorses Dehler*

Another painful late blow came the Wednesday before the election when the *St. Cloud Times* endorsed my opponent. This was the only daily newspaper in the region and the only media outlet of any kind that made endorsements in the race. I had gone in for my endorsement interview with the editorial board a few weeks earlier. The conversation had gone very well, and I was hopeful for the endorsement. The brief endorsement editorial read as follows:

> College professor Jim Read may be more knowledgeable about the complex issues that will face the legislature and doesn't back away from controversial stands, but St. Joseph Mayor Steve Dehler has roots on his side. A lifelong resident of his district and a longtime activist in local government, he has a better sense of who his constituents are and what values best represent them.

One of my supporters, Jeanne Cook, responded with a letter to the editor that was published the Sunday before the election. She wrote, "The Times admits that Jim Read is 'more knowledgeable about the complex issues that will face the legislature' but endorses his opponent because he is a lifelong resident of his district.... As one who was born and raised in Stearns County, I am insulted by this backward attitude of 'us' versus 'them.' I want to be represented by the most knowledgeable, not the most local candidate."

As it turns out, just over a year later Pia was hired as the editorial page editor of the *St. Cloud Times* and subsequently sat regularly on the other side of endorsement interviews and the internal politics behind endorsement decisions. Her retrospective translation of the paper's endorsement editorial for Dehler is as follows: "Read is the better candidate, but he doesn't stand a chance in rural Stearns County. We're not going to waste our political influence endorsing a candidate who can't win."

Get Out the Vote!

We had no shortage of volunteers for our get-out-the-vote efforts. What we lacked was a large and conveniently accessible list of likely prospects to call. There was no good list of self-identified Democrats living in the district because in Minnesota voters do not publicly state their party affiliation when they vote in a primary. The state party could not provide us with any worthwhile information on our district; our own lists were much better than theirs.

We did have some information from the limited UDF phone survey operations conducted in our district (see chapter 3) and from our own phone surveys, but together these surveys had generated information on less than a tenth of the eligible voters (which would represent less than a fifth of the households) in the district. A potentially much larger source of information was my own handwritten door-knocking notes, because I had contacted approximately three-quarters of the households in the district. In that way I had generated my own list of definite and likely supporters. But we never had time to translate my door-knocking information into a database accessible to anyone else. I consulted my own door-knocking notes when I made phone calls; given a name and address from a registered voters list, I could often track down whether I had spoken to the person and how he or she had responded to me. (Of course, there was a lot of guesswork in generating a list of supporters from my notes; some voters are more revealing than others.) My unaided memory of a contact was also pretty reliable. But I could not personally call thousands of households in the four days preceding the election (even if I were not spending time and energy on last-minute mailings), and my handwritten notes were not in a form immediately usable by volunteers. Instead, I would rifle through my notes and tell volunteers sitting in the room who I believed should or should not be called. On the whole ours was a well-organized campaign, but on this point we clearly fell short.

Where we did have good phone survey information, our get-out-the-vote calling proceeded in the following order. First, we called clearly identified Jim Read supporters from the survey lists, my door-knocking records, or other sources. This was finished pretty quickly (any campaign volunteer could handle this task), and many of these people were contacted more than once. We then moved on to the larger group of voters who in the UDF surveys had declared themselves undecided on my legislative race. These we contacted in the following rank order: first, anyone who said they were voting for Bill Clinton and leaned Democratic; then self-described independents who identified themselves as pro-choice or "in-between" on the abortion issue. (We assumed that self-identified pro-choice voters would consider me the lesser evil compared to my opponent.) Then we proceeded to Democrats and independents who declared themselves pro-life but undecided in the legislative race (which suggested they were not single-issue voters). As we moved down the priority list, we were obviously shifting from pure get-out-the-vote calls to last-minute persuasion calls. Our most effective volunteers and I handled the persuasion calls. Of course we did not call anyone who said they were supporting my opponent or any self-identified pro-life Republicans. I believe we made good use of the limited pool of survey information we had. When we had completely exhausted all voters for whom we had survey information, we began calling from a registered voters list in precincts I considered good territory.

We also did a targeted mailing to the modestly sized list of self-identified Jim Read supporters. The mailing was a large red postcard with "Jim Read for State Representative" on one side and on the reverse side the address of that person's polling location, along with a map, and reminder of the date of the election and polling hours. Pia and Peg McGlinch (walking through a snowstorm the night before the election) also lit-dropped this same postcard in St. Joseph and a few other places we considered good territory.

Minnesota has one of the highest rates of voter turnout in the United States, and turnout in our district was typically pretty robust. The presidential race would of course boost turnout, and so might a hotly contested Seventh District congressional race featuring a local (and Republican) challenger. Beyond our limited list of identified Jim Read supporters and self-identified local Democrats, we would have to depend on many voters about whom we had no information getting to the polls for their own reasons and voting for me because I had made a good impression on them sometime in the last six months.

Turning Out the Student Vote

Turning out the student vote at the College of St. Benedict and St. John's University students who lived in apartments in St. Joseph presented challenges of a different kind. A large proportion of the students would be voting for the first time in their lives. Those who took an interest in the 1992 election tended to be motivated by the presidential campaign; a state legislative race was even further from the typical student voter's thoughts than from those of other voters in the district. No phone surveys were done with students so it was difficult to generate a list of supporters to turn out on election day. (Students' campus phone numbers were not public information, and for me as a faculty member to use the in-house directory for a massive phone campaign would be a conflict of interest.) Most students were away from campus during the summer and returned to St. Joseph just at the point when our campaign became overloaded with other pressing matters.

Of course, as a professor on campus every day I had some visibility and name recognition. And I had a natural rapport with college students that my opponent lacked. But I could not campaign from in front of my classroom; teaching and running for office were separate roles, and I was careful not to mix them. I spoke on campus as a candidate only as guest speaker in other professors' classes and in out-of-class gatherings organized by students active in my campaign. I did not personally door-knock the College of St. Benedict dormitories, even though as a candidate for office I had a legal right to do so. (Student volunteers did work the dormitories for me.) Given scarcity of time and my daily presence on campus as a faculty member, I believed my door-knocking hours were better spent in Sartell or Avon or Albany than on campus. And if the off-campus community were to perceive me as ignoring their concerns in order to court the student vote — if I were pegged as simply "the College of St. Benedict's candidate" — then I was done for.

Through most of the campaign I depended on Peg McGlinch and a few other really effective student volunteers to organize for me on campus. But actually turning out the student vote on election day required considerable planning and resources from our campaign. Minnesota, unlike most states, allows for election day voter registration. This is a great potential boon for college student voters, most of whom miss the deadline for preregistration. But many students do not know that they can register on election day. Many others do not know they can declare their college town as their voting residence, believing incorrectly that they can only vote where their parents live. (This misapprehension is sometimes deliberately encouraged by local elites who do not want students "interfering" in their elections.) In the weeks leading up to the election we placed full-page ads in the student newspapers describing when and where students could vote and what identification they would need to register on election day. Our ad assured students that "you have a RIGHT to vote here in St. Joseph" and emphasized it would be a close election where "College of St. Benedict students may determine the winner."

On election day itself the challenge was actually getting students to the polls when most had no idea where the polling place was. In previous election years there had been an on-campus polling place for St. Joseph Precinct 3 (composed of the college and St. Benedict's monastery). But for some reason the city of St. Joseph eliminated Precinct 3 just before the 1992 election. (Precinct 3 was restored in later election years.) Students were now expected to find their way across town to City Hall, an obscure little edifice hiding behind the fire station. There was additional confusion because upper-class students who had voted on campus at Precinct 3 in 1990 were expecting to do so again and in many cases inadvertently misinformed their younger classmates on this point. It was clear that if we did not intervene, the student turnout would be low in spite of widespread student interest in the presidential election.

With what Pia describes as "the best money we ever spent," we rented a van to drive students (and monastics) from Mary Commons in the middle of campus to City Hall to vote. She decked out the van with a big sign saying, "RIDES TO THE POLLS." Minnesota election law prohibits any campaign signs or literature or any kind of electioneering in vehicles transporting voters to polling places. Our campaign drove anyone to the polls who wanted to go, including many Republicans (as Pia could tell from overhearing conversations). Pia drove back and forth between campus and polls all day, and the van was full every time. The City Hall polling place (apparently planning on a lower student turnout) ran out of ballots long before the polls were closed and had to send away for more.

A Peculiar Interpretation of Law

It snowed heavily the day and night before the election. Of course we were nervous about what effect the snow would have on turnout and which candidates, if any, would be disadvantaged by it. Pia's election day photos of the St. Joseph American Legion Post show about a foot of wet snow on the ground.

She took these photos for a specific reason: to prove that my opponent was violating election law by posting campaign signs too close to the polling place. Minnesota election law prohibits any electioneering or campaign signs within one hundred feet of a polling place on election day. In the days leading up to the election my opponent had posted seven large Steve Dehler signs within fifty feet of both of the St. Joseph polling places; on election day two of the signs had "Vote Today" stickers attached.

The law would seem to be pretty clear. Pia had called Dehler the night before the election to request that he remove the signs before the polls opened, citing Chapter 211B.11, Subsection 1 of Minnesota statutes. The catch was that my opponent owned the property across the street from the two polling places, and he did not believe the law obligated him to remove campaign signs from his own property. He also argued that because the signs had been put up *before* election day, not *on* election day, it was legal to keep them up. He refused to remove the signs. At 7:10 a.m. on election day Pia filed a formal complaint with the St. Joseph elections judge—who also happened to be my opponent's campaign treasurer. She supported my opponent's interpretation of the law. By midmorning Pia had contacted the Stearns County sheriff's department and the Stearns County attorney, neither of whom was willing to direct my opponent to take down the signs. By the end of the day Pia had contacted a lawyer who worked for the Minnesota DFL Party (and who later represented my campaign in the recount) who supported our interpretation of the law. Pia was doing all this in between shuttling students back and forth in the van and coordinating all our other get-out-the-vote efforts.

The DFL lawyer later told us that we had a good case, and I could formally challenge the election results if I chose, but I would have to be able to argue convincingly that my opponent's violation of election law was substantial enough to affect the outcome of the election. Assuming that I won that point, the remedy would have been to nullify the election results and hold a special election for the seat. Given the election results in those two precincts (Read 732, Dehler 407 in Precinct 1; Read 388, Dehler 278 in Precinct 2), it would be difficult to persuade people that his signs cost me the election. And even if I won that point, voter irritation at having to show up for a special election would probably not have weighed in my favor.

The truth of the matter is that Pia and I were so worked up, on edge, and sleep-deprived by election day that our nervous energy needed an outlet, and my opponent's signs served as that outlet. I am convinced to this day that he infringed the law, but the matter was of miniscule significance compared to everything else that occurred in the campaign. We laugh now about the magnitude of our righteous indignation over a few signs. The best thing that came out of the fracas is that we now have several photographs of the town in which I lived and worked as it looked on that significant day in our lives.

Election Day and a Long Night

Election day for me was a frenzied blur, and I can retain few details now. I know I voted, because Pia took a photo of me coming out of the ballot booth, but I cannot now bring to life my only experience of marking my own name on the ballot. I know I was shaking hands at the Sartell post office at noon only because I recall someone's praising me for doing so, not because I remember it myself. I must have taught classes but have no recollection of doing so.

Our election night gathering was at the El Paso in St. Joseph (a combination restaurant, bar, and bowling alley; election reports were punctuated by the noise of falling bowling pins). Pia was away for most of the evening because she had agreed to work for the Voter News Service, coordinating a team of students gathering selected precinct results for the presidential and congressional races. We knew results for my race would be slow in coming and that any decision would come well past midnight. My supporters and I did have the pleasure of toasting Bill Clinton's victory early in the evening.

News about my own race depended on how quickly precinct results were communicated to the auditor's offices of three separate counties, and when those offices chose to disclose it to us over the phone. We got the St. Joseph results early and were pleased with my large margin. I was even more pleased to learn that I had won Sartell, a Republican-leaning city in which I had campaigned energetically. I was breaking even or narrowly ahead in several large townships (Brockway and St. Wendel). I was behind in Republican strongholds like Le Sauk and Avon townships and the city of Albany, but doing better than usual for a Democrat. When we went to bed (though not to sleep) after midnight, I had a narrow lead, but we had not yet heard from Morrison County or the more rural and conservative Stearns County precincts like Krain Township.

By about six in the morning we learned that I had not won the election. Losing by large margins several rural precincts like Krain Township (246 to 119) and Elmdale Township in Morrison County (213 to 135) had nullified my early lead from St. Joseph and Sartell. The extent of my reported loss was magnified by a reporting error, so that my opponent was reported in the next day's *St. Cloud Times* as winning by 286 votes, too large a margin for a recount. By Thursday the error was corrected, and the reported margin was now 93 votes. Minnesota law provides for automatic, state-funded recounts in legislative races decided by fewer than 200 votes. The recount was scheduled for November 23–25 at the Stearns County auditor's office.

I did not hold any high hopes for the recount. Barring discovery of fraud or major mechanical malfunctions, a 93-vote margin was unlikely to be reversed. Votes would change, but the changes were unlikely to all fall my way. A long series of coin tosses is unlikely to produce all heads or all tails.

Midway between the election and the recount I delivered a political theory paper on "The Possibility and Limits of Expanded Participation" to the Northeastern Political Science Association in Providence, Rhode Island. How I found time and concentration to write this paper I have no idea.

Discerning Voter Intent

The pile of ballots lay on a table. Seated at the table was an election official. Standing on either side and looking over the official's shoulders were attorneys hired by the legislative caucuses to represent the Republican and Democratic candidates. We the candidates were also entitled to be present, but we were silent players in the show. Pia stood in for me during the first two days of the recount; I was present the last day, when the judgment was announced.

The election official would turn over each ballot, and both attorneys would look at it. If either attorney challenged the ballot, it would be set aside for later resolution. After the challenged ballots had been set aside, the unchallenged ballots were counted. Then examination of the challenged ballots would begin. Some of the precincts in the district used optical scan machines to read ballots, but many (perhaps most) precincts still used hand-counted paper ballots. There were fortunately no punch card ballots and consequently no hanging chads.

There were many reasons why a particular ballot might be questioned. A voter might, for instance, have marked one candidate, then crossed it out and marked another, initialing the change. An optical scan machine would reject such a ballot as an "overvote" (voting for both candidates), and precinct election judges counting ballots by hand might reject such a ballot for the same reason. But a recount allows for the rejected ballot to be reconsidered and for the attorneys to discern and debate the voter's intent. Or a voter (perhaps elderly and frail) might have marked the ballot with scratchings too thin and light for a machine to register. The election official would hear the arguments on both sides and make the final decision on each questionable ballot.

Another type of challenged ballot occurred when the voter wrote some kind of text over the face of the ballot sheet. For instance, a voter might register a discernible vote in all the contests on the ballot, then write in the margin: "They all suck!" If the handwritten text was too close to the spot where a vote is to be marked, an optical scan machine might reject the ballot. During a manual recount such a remark causes uncertainties of a different kind. Does "They all suck!" mean that the voter has retroactively canceled all of his or her votes and chosen not to vote as an act of protest? Or is the remark to be interpreted merely as an expression of a general attitude with no intended effect on the individual's vote? Attorneys engage in learned arguments over such matters.

During the high-stakes manual recount of the presidential vote in Florida in 2000, some columnists and TV pundits railed sarcastically at the very notion of discerning voter intent, as though this were some new and dubious procedure for recounts. In my own recount, discerning voter intent was the standard embodied in law and accepted by both sides, and it guided debate over any challenged ballot. I do not know what other standard could have been employed.

The recount changed in one way or another more than one hundred votes, enough to win me the election if they had all fallen my way, but of course they did not. The most significant changes were not reversed votes (votes originally counted for Dehler that went to Read or vice versa) but votes not included at all in the initial count that were added as a result of the recount. I picked up twenty-two additional votes, and my opponent picked up twenty-seven. The recount thus increased his margin of victory from ninety-three to ninety-eight votes. The final result after recount was Dehler, 7,576 (50.3 percent); Read, 7,478 (49.7 percent).

Door Knocking Seems to Work

After the election several people remarked to me, "Wasn't it devastating to work so hard and then lose by so narrow a margin?" To this I answered no. If I had worked so hard and then been blown out, *that* would have been devastating. To lose by ninety-eight votes was bittersweet.

People would also sometimes remark that the voters of the district must be idiots to elect Dehler over me: "They deserve what they get." But my perspective on this is very different. This was a Republican district. The Democratic legislative candidate in 1990 had received 32 percent of the vote; the 1988 candidate got 41 percent. That I pulled this up to 49.7 percent suggests that many voters who might otherwise vote for a Republican responded positively to me and to the type of campaign I ran. The cities and townships where I did comparatively well in the election results were by and large the ones that I had door-knocked most intensively. Where I lost the election was in the most distant and sparsely populated townships, places neither my opponent nor I spent much time campaigning. In these regions the default behavior of the voters was heavily in his favor.

I believe that my door knocking paid off and persuaded many people to vote for me who would not have otherwise. It would be difficult to prove this conclusively. (I was not about to door-knock some precincts and leave other, comparable precincts untouched in order to conduct a controlled experiment on the effects of door knocking.) But this conclusion is suggested by comparison of my performance with that of other Democratic candidates in 1992 and earlier years.

It is tricky to compare a two-way legislative contest with a three-way presidential race, but the comparison is nevertheless revealing. In District 14A George H. W. Bush finished on top with 38 percent, followed by Bill Clinton with 35 percent, and Ross Perot with 26 percent. Statewide, Clinton won Minnesota with 43.5 percent followed by Bush (31.9 percent) and Perot (24 percent). Thus, the district in which I ran voted six to eight percentage points more Republican than the state as a whole in the 1992 presidential contest. I did not run away from the national ticket as many Democrats did who ran for office in conservative regions. But I was definitely not riding any Clinton coattails in District 14A. (I should note in passing that both Clinton and Perot were pro-choice and together got 61 percent of the vote even in my very conservative district; this challenges the MCCL claim that there was an unquestioned pro-life consensus in our community.)

The Seventh District congressional contest was a two-way race, but comparison is difficult for another reason: the Republican challenger, Bernie Omann, was the outgoing legislative incumbent and thus a kind of "favorite son" in the congressional race. In the Seventh District as a whole, the one-term Democratic incumbent Collin Peterson defeated Omann by a narrow margin. But in District 14A, Omann outpolled Peterson 68 percent to 32 percent. Thus, I was definitely not riding any Peterson coattails either. It is worth noting that a significant number of voters in the district voted for Omann for Congress and me for state legislature, despite Omann's public endorsement of my opponent.

Turnout overall in the Read-Dehler contest, measured as a percentage of the 22,683 adults of voting age living in District 14A, was about 66 percent. Intriguingly there were 478 more total votes cast in the Read-Dehler race than were cast in the Seventh District congressional race in 14A, in which 64 percent of voting-age adults participated. Turnout for the presidential race in the district was about 68 percent.

The effectiveness of my door knocking is perhaps better demonstrated by examining some particular cities and precincts. I energetically door-knocked St. Joseph, the town where both candidates lived and where my

Election results, 1992, Minnesota House District 14A

City/Township	President			Congress		Minnesota House 14A	
	Bush (R)	Clinton (D)	Perot (Reform)	Omann (R)	Peterson (D)	Dehler (R)	Read (D)
Albany	395	228	202	616	210	449	350
Albany Township	154	84	128	265	100	191	163
Avon	190	163	124	355	127	253	221
Avon Township	373	270	281	640	283	498	420
Brockway Township	380	370	382	749	387	552	565
Holding Township	179	184	166	382	151	261	267
Holdingford	118	130	75	225	100	180	140
Krain Township	158	79	118	283	88	246	119
Le Sauk Township	511	357	270	805	329	625	503
Pleasant Lake	23	20	23	45	22	40	26
St. Anthony	14	14	6	24	10	16	19
St. Joseph	635	996	344	953	766	687	1,121
St. Joseph Township	413	346	282	678	328	526	490
St. Stephen	167	92	109	269	106	211	164
St. Wendel Township	381	334	283	646	354	493	500
Sartell	779	651	435	1,229	577	854	951
Stearns County	4,870	4,318	3,228	8,164	3,938	6,082	6,019
	39%	35%	26%	67%	33%	50%	50%
Bellevue Township	179	118	115	286	124	223	174
Bowlus	41	55	47	115	28	81	57
Elmdale	6	26	19	37	16	27	26
Elmdale Township	131	116	108	251	109	213	135
Royalton	153	121	106	273	101	198	167
Swan River Township	100	182	87	245	125	133	215
Two Rivers Township	97	85	80	207	61	157	104
Upsala	96	90	41	151	82	119	107
Morrison County	803	793	603	1,565	646	1,151	985
	37%	36%	27%	71%	29%	54%	46%
Rice	87	94	82	N/A	N/A	118	138
Sartell (East)	206	250	163	157	106	225	336
Benton County	293	344	245	157	106	343	474
	33%	39%	28%	60%	40%	42%	58%
District 14A total	5,966	5,455	4,076	9,886	4,690	7,576	7,478
	38%	35%	26%	68%	32%	50.3%	49.7%

Source: Election Division, Minnesota Secretary of State

opponent was the incumbent mayor. It is probably not surprising that I won by a large margin in the St. Joseph precinct that included the college (and also half of the city). But I also won by a healthy margin in the city precinct that did not include the college. Overall, I won St. Joseph 1,121 to 687.

St. Joseph tends to vote Democratic anyway (my opponent had won a nonpartisan mayoral election), so my margin there might not be entirely attributable to my door knocking. Sartell, the largest city in the district, more strongly suggests the effectiveness of my door knocking. I door-knocked the entire city twice and had more extended doorstep conversations with voters there than anywhere else. The city leans Republican, but more in a Twin Cities–suburban than traditional Stearns County way. I defeated my opponent in Sartell 1,287 to 1,079 (or 54 percent to 46 percent). In the presidential race Bush led Sartell with 985 votes followed by Clinton's 901 and Perot's 598. In the congressional race the Republican candidate Omann got 1,386 votes (67 percent) in Sartell to the Democratic incumbent Peterson's 683 (33 percent).

I also door-knocked Albany twice, the third-largest city in the district after Sartell and St. Joseph. This was much more conservative territory than St. Joseph or Sartell. My opponent defeated me 449 to 350 in Albany. But this was a strong performance compared to other Democratic candidates. Bush carried Albany with 395 votes to Clinton's distant 228 and Perot's 202. Omann defeated Peterson 616 to 210 in Albany. Other conservative regions that I door-knocked energetically, such as Avon, Avon Township, Albany Township, Le Sauk Township, and Royalton, tell a similar story: I did not come out ahead, but I was not far behind.

The argument for the effectiveness of door knocking can also be made negatively by examining results in precincts I did not get to at all or very little. I did spend one long day driving from one remote farm to another in Krain Township, but it would have taken me five days to cover it adequately. (I do not have access to my opponent's campaign schedule, but I doubt he was out there more than I was.) I lost Krain Township 246 to 119, a margin (127 votes) significantly larger than the 98 votes by which I lost the election as a whole. Dehler's two to one advantage over me in Krain roughly mirrors Bush's margin over Clinton in Krain Township (158 to 79; Perot with 118 did much better than Clinton). In Krain Township, in other words, I was treated like any other Democratic candidate. (My 32.6 percent there did outperform Collin Peterson's 23.7 percent.) Elmdale Township, Bellevue Township, and Two Rivers Township in Morrison County tell a similar story: I campaigned there very little or not at all. None of these was a highly populated precinct, but losing a small precinct by a large margin has a large impact in a close election.

I do need to admit one exception to my argument for the success of my door knocking. I door-knocked Holdingford pretty energetically, and historically it had been only one of two reliable Democratic towns in the district (St. Joseph was the other). But I lost Holdingford 180 to 140. This was one of the few cities where Clinton outpolled Bush (Clinton, 130; Bush, 118; Perot, 75) and where my own relative performance lagged behind Clinton's. I do know that the pro-lifers were very effectively organized against me in Holdingford, despite my door knocking. I have found that some pro-life Democrats will tolerate a pro-choice presidential candidate but want a pro-lifer representing their community in St. Paul. I also was not at my best at the Holdingford candidate forum when faced with a series of hostile antiabortion questions. My problem in Holdingford was not that I was unknown. The problem was that they looked at me and decided they did not support me. Door knocking is not a panacea.

The argument for the effectiveness of my door knocking would of course be complicated if my opponent had door-knocked as much as I had and in the same places. In that case we would not be comparing more door knocking against less, but comparing the *quality* of doorstep contacts by different candidates, which would be much more difficult to assess. I cannot determine with any precision how much my opponent door-knocked and where. I can only report from circumstantial evidence that he door-knocked far less than I did, and that activists in his own party were worried that he was not door-knocking enough.

I can report with more certainty that our 1990 Democratic legislative candidate door-knocked very little, because I was party chair at the time. He was challenging an incumbent rather than running for an open seat as I did. But he made a good in-person impression, and I suspect that he would have received better than 32 percent of the vote if he had door-knocked seriously.

Bernie Omann, the outgoing legislative incumbent now running for Congress, was himself very energetic in his door knocking. Once during the summer when I was campaigning near St. Stephen, I ran into him at his mother's house. He seemed impressed by my door knocking and claimed that in 1988 (his first regular campaign for the legislative seat) he had visited every household in the district. If he had run for reelection to the legislature instead of running for Congress, he would have matched me door for door, and I doubt I would have come as close.

I believe my work paid off and that voters at the doors listened to what I was saying. This is why I was not devastated by my narrow defeat and why I do not believe voters in the district were idiots for electing my opponent. The results would have been very different if voters' decisions had been overwhelmingly determined by party affiliation or by a tight community's prejudice against an outsider; in that case I would not have come close. I was not able to reach every voter in person, and I cannot hold it against the voters I did not reach that receiving an occasional mailing from me or glancing at one of my yard signs did not swing them my way. I believe the voters I was able to reach in person by and large gave me a fair hearing. I persuaded many to vote for me in a district not favorable to Democrats. Many others heard me out, understood my position on key issues, and made a considered judgment in favor of my opponent. This was unfortunate from my perspective, but it hardly makes them fools.

The reader should recall that I became a candidate in the first place because no one else was willing to run. As a recently elected local party chair I would have been ashamed if we could not even field a candidate. As a citizen and teacher of politics, I considered it essential that voters have a genuine choice in elections rather than mere token opposition or no opposition at all. My original reason for becoming a candidate was to ensure the viability of our local Democratic Party at a time when it was in danger of crumbling, and to give voters in the district a genuine choice among clearly distinguishable candidates in a community where it was too often pretended that everyone thought alike. I believe in both cases I can say I succeeded.

Recovery and Aftershock

What I recall most clearly about the months following the election was our rediscovering the joys of a normal private and social life. We could now go out to dinner with friends and talk about something besides my campaign. We could go away for weekends or spend a week in the Boundary Waters. We were glad I had run and relieved it was over.

The campaign did not easily let go of us, however. In the months following the election I would occasionally get calls from people whose houses I had visited during the campaign who assumed I had been elected and who had some constituent service request. By campaigning so energetically I had "bonded" with a significant portion of residents of the district—including some who did not closely follow election news—and this bonding effect did not dissipate immediately. The controversy stirred up by my position on abortion continued in the op-ed section of local newspapers for a while after the election. I also continued to get letters and phone calls related to abortion. Some of these communications were worthy of a reply despite the fact that I was no longer a candidate. Some were not.

The largest aftershock of my campaign came almost four years later, as the result of a strange series of events involving incumbent District 14 state senator Joe Bertram of Paynesville and his brother, District 14B state representative Jeff Bertram. The reader may recall that both Bertrams kept their distance from the Democratic Party and were in substance conservative independents with their own base of support owing little to the party. Neither of the Bertrams was especially effective or respected as legislators at the state capitol, but at home in the district they had built up an impressive political machine through energetic constituent service and, at times, through alleged intimidation of critics and opponents.[1]

In September 1995 Joe Bertram was caught shoplifting from a local store whose owner had been suspicious for some time and had directed

employees to watch him. A Senate Ethics Committee investigation un-
covered that Bertram had compounded the offense by allegedly trying to
buy the store owner's silence. (Jeff Bertram had allegedly also put pressure
on the shop owner to drop the matter.) Joe Bertram fought for a while to
save his position but resigned in January 1996.

I had no role in Joe Bertram's downfall other than to recruit and work
for a Democratic candidate hoping to fill his seat in the special election.
But Bertram's downfall caused a number of people who had hitherto kept
silent about the Bertram dynasty to speak up publicly. This led to public
accusations against Jeff Bertram that did have some connection to me.

Jeff Bertram was accused by a surprisingly large number of people of
verbally or physically threatening them and of fabricating vicious rumors
about individuals who crossed him. "Witnesses have told the House Ethics Committee about Jeff Bertram trying to force his way into an Albany
radio station and threatening to give his advertising to another salesman
if his usual one didn't donate $100 to his campaign. Others described him
spreading a false rumor that the clerk who caught his brother shoplifting was dating a young man who was high on drugs when he caused the
deaths of three townspeople in a car accident."[2] Many other accusations
surfaced in the course of a House Ethics Committee investigation and were
reported in the newspapers.

The reader may recall from chapter 5 that when Jeff Bertram withdrew
his letter of endorsement on October 20, 1992, he had also told me he
would get back at the Republican activist who had leaked the existence of
the letter (triggering a massive abortion-related pressure campaign against
Bertram that endangered his career). Bertram had claimed (falsely) that
this individual was being investigated for molestation and said he would
start spreading this news around. I had asked him not to do this, fearing
that I would somehow be implicated in a slander campaign. I believed I
had persuaded him not to do this. All of this occurred in October 1992.

But when details of the House Ethics Committee hearings started to
become public in the early months of 1996, I was floored to read in the
newspaper that the committee had heard accusations that Jeff Bertram had
slandered exactly this same Republican activist, in exactly the same way
that Bertram had threatened to do when I spoke with him on the phone on

October 20, 1992. He had executed precisely the revenge he had promised me he would not do. The results of the Ethics Committee hearing made it clear that the behavior I had witnessed four years before was not an isolated instance but a pattern, a deliberate technique.

At this point I decided I had to speak up about what I knew. Bertram was claiming that all of these accusations were merely a partisan scheme on the part of Republicans who wanted to pick up his legislative seat. I was in a position to know that at least one of the accusations was not false. And as a former Democratic Party chair and legislative candidate I could not be credibly accused of participating in Republican conspiracies. I had also directly witnessed at least one instance in which Bertram had invented and circulated malicious rumors to intimidate local Democrats who challenged him. I decided to invite myself to testify before the Minnesota House Ethics Committee.

The DFL Party enjoyed at the time a majority in both House and Senate. The ethics procedure in the senate was designed in a way that made it easier for Democrats to investigate alleged offenses by a member of their own party. Ethics procedures in the House (at least at the time) unfortunately left it up to the Republican leadership to bring ethics charges against Democratic legislators (and vice versa). So to tell the Ethics Committee what I knew about Jeff Bertram's past behavior, I took the initiative to contact Rep. Steve Sviggum, the Republican minority leader, who in turn put me in contact with Rep. Charlie Weaver (also Republican), who was conducting the investigation into the ethics charges against Bertram. I worked well with both Sviggum and Weaver in preparing my testimony. Rep. Dee Long, the Democratic speaker of the House in 1992, who knew about the withdrawn letter, also encouraged me to go forward with my testimony.

On March 15, 1996, I testified before the House Ethics Committee. In my prepared testimony I described what Jeff Bertram had said to me over the phone on October 20, 1992 (I had kept my campaign phone records) and another incident involving harassment of local Democrats that occurred on October 30, 1995 (during fallout over Joe Bertram's shoplifting episode). After reporting the two incidents in detail with supporting documents, I went on in my testimony to explain why I believed this kind of behavior by an elected official threatened the integrity of the democratic process. I observed that the local Republican activist was simply doing his job in leaking the letter and organizing pro-life pressure against Jeff Bertram; this was within the rules of ordinary party politics, and I would have done the same thing in his situation. But Jeff Bertram's retaliation was far beyond the bounds of ordinary politics:

> I know some people will say that personal attacks and rumors are an ordinary part of politics. But . . . in small towns and rural communities rumors travel fast. People's very livelihood often depends upon their reputation in the community. A false and malicious rumor deliberately circulated by an elected representative is likely to reach more people, and do more damage, than a charge made in print where at least you could hold someone responsible for what they say. . . . And legislators are not ordinary links in the gossip chain. They speak to far more people, and normally their word is given more credit, than the average purveyor of gossip. They have far more power and therefore can do far more harm than the ordinary person can.

On the day I testified I heard other testimony about what Jeff Bertram had done to this same individual. I cannot estimate the number of people to whom Bertram communicated the slander, but judging from other witnesses at the Ethics Committee hearing, newspaper accounts, and my own subsequent queries in the district, I am convinced the number was not small. I believe Bertram set out to destroy permanently this person's public and private reputation in retaliation for an ordinary act of political opposition.[3]

In response to the argument that the voters should decide whether and how to punish Jeff Bertram, I replied that this argument "makes sense only where people are free to criticize their elected officials and oppose them politically without fear of losing their reputation and their livelihood. Jeff Bertram has created a hostile climate in which there is no room for ordinary political opposition and hence no democracy." (It should be recalled here that Bertram was literally unopposed for reelection in 1990 and 1992.

A local Republican activist who has organized an effective pressure campaign might be a prospective future electoral rival. One begins to wonder whether factors other than universal admiration explained the dearth of electoral challengers.)

I agreed that Jeff Bertram should be expelled from the legislature. The resolution to expel him received a slim majority (all the Republicans and a few Democrats voting to expel) but failed to get the required two-thirds majority. A DFL-sponsored vote of censure did pass.[4] Several Democratic legislators later told me they acknowledged the serious character of Bertram's offenses but considered expulsion too extreme a remedy.

Some Democratic legislators and staffers were angry with me for going after a Democrat at a time when the party clung to a slim majority in the house. But back in the district I was applauded by many local Democrats who were ashamed by the actions of both Bertrams and wanted to clean house. Shortly after I testified against Jeff Bertram I was elected again as local DFL Party chair (a position I had resigned when I ran for office in 1992). My election as chair was a signal that the local party wanted someone new. Shortly thereafter Jeff Bertram reversed course and announced that he would not run for reelection. We found a good Democratic candidate to take his place, but the 14B seat was won by a young Republican and former student of mine, Doug Stang.

In this book I have argued that direct personal communications between legislators (or candidates) and ordinary voters are essential to a healthy democracy. But not every in-person communication contributes to political health. Both Joe and Jeff Bertram were adept in the art of personal politicking. They worked hard, got around, talked to lots of people, and gained many voters' trust—trust that in some significant instances was abused. For a candidate to converse about abortion, health care, education funding, taxes and so on with individual voters at their doorsteps promotes civic engagement and the habits of democracy. Using those same personal meetings to spread deliberately damaging rumors about political opponents and personal enemies definitely does not promote civic engagement or democracy. Every power can be abused, and the power generated by face-to-face interaction with voters is no exception.

But the nature of politics abhors a vacuum. If people who believe in healthy civic engagement do not foster it beyond the narrow circle of their own acquaintances, if they consider the business of politics — or at least local politics — to be beneath them, then the tone of political life in the community will be set by someone else, for good or ill. If anyone reading this sordid episode of slander and political revenge feels this is one more reason to stay away from local politics, I would encourage them to draw exactly the opposite conclusion.

Why I Did Not Run Again

A candidate who loses a very close election is an obvious prospect to run again, and many people encouraged me to do so. But though I stayed active and as party chair successfully recruited other legislative candidates in following years, I never again ran for the legislature myself.

There were many particular reasons for this. (I could pretend I knew 1994 would not be a good year for Democrats, but I was not that prescient.) I was scheduled to apply for tenure and my first sabbatical in fall 1994. Running for office again would have drained time away from my teaching when I needed to demonstrate excellence as a teacher. And I was ambitious to establish myself as a political theorist and scholar of American political thought. I had begun campaigning for office right on the tails of a yearlong research fellowship for which I had not yet produced any finished product. Years later I came to appreciate how my practical political experience had enriched me both as a teacher and as a political theorist. But immediately after the campaign I felt that professionally I had taken a very time-consuming detour and it would take all my energy to get back on track.

In late 1993 Pia was hired as editorial page editor of the *St. Cloud Times* and discovered her true calling as an opinion writer. When we moved to Stearns County in 1988, it was not clear how in central Minnesota she could build upon her Peace Corps experience and her master's degree from the Fletcher School of Law and Diplomacy. But her intensive involvement in state and local politics combined with her education to make her one of most intelligent and respected editorial writers in the state, and her professional star rose quickly. This meant, however, that she would not be available to manage my campaign if I ran again; indeed, any public involvement would have compromised her position at the newspaper. I doubted I could find anyone as good to manage a campaign in her place.

Beyond all these particular reasons, however, was one big reason. Running for elective office had not been part of my life plan before 1992. My decision to run for the legislature signified at the same time a radical shift in my (our) life plans. If I had won the election, I would have put my old life plans aside and adopted this new life for a decade (or as long as the voters tolerated me). Either life plan would have satisfied me. But it is difficult and disorienting to keep switching back and forth. When I came close but did not win, I went back to my original life plans and professional ambitions, and I have kept to them, for better or worse, ever since.

Two other considerations deserve mention. First, I never considered the experience of running for office to have been pointless or a failure simply because I did not win. For that reason I never felt compelled to run again simply to recoup the time and passion I had invested in the first campaign. I learned a great deal about myself and the world and had an impact on the community even without winning the election. But I believe these compensations come only if you run with the intention of winning, doing everything you can to converse with voters and persuade them to support you. Just putting your name on the ballot accomplishes little.

Second, I never considered myself the only good legislative candidate living within the boundaries of the district. I never pretended to be "the indispensable man." In my closing statement at the St. Joseph candidate forum on October 6, 1992, I remarked that if elected, I would limit myself to ten years in the office. "There are many of you out here tonight who can also do this job well. It should be a citizen legislature. And there should be people out here tonight who have the ambition to do the kind of thing that Steve and I are doing this year." Even as a candidate for office I was encouraging others to participate in our democracy as candidates for office. That was what I was doing before I ran for office, and I continued doing it when my own campaign was over.

The District and Party since 1992

I became a candidate in 1992 because as DFL chair I had been trying to build an active and vital local Democratic Party in challenging territory. I ran for office myself because I could not persuade anyone else to run, and inability to field a candidate would have meant our party-building efforts had failed. I did not win the election. And I cannot claim that our local party enjoyed spectacular electoral success in District 14 over the next decade. None of our DFL candidates in 14A came as close in 1994, 1996, 1998, or 2000 as I did in 1992. But all of them did much better than our candidates had in 1988 and 1990. All those who followed me were good candidates, though I do not believe any of them door-knocked as much as I did in 1992. My campaign at least proved that a Democrat could be competitive in 14A, and we never let Dehler go unchallenged for reelection. In District 14B and in Senate District 14—which became my responsibilities when I was elected District 14 DFL chair again in 1996—we fielded some very good candidates over the years and some less impressive ones. The Republicans who had replaced Joe and Jeff Bertram, Michelle Fischbach in Senate District 14 and Doug Stang in House District 14B, were able to hold those seats. From 1992 until 2004 (after redistricting had changed the boundaries), Republicans had a lock on District 14's legislative delegation.

Thus, our party-building effort might appear a failure. But in fact it was a success if judged by the standard of political participation rather than immediate electoral success. My 1990–92 initiatives as party chair and my 1992 campaign helped energize many new or renewed Democrats, who remained active in the years that followed. I do not claim exclusive credit for this jump in participation; there were dozens of great activists, and my campaign was as much effect as cause of this participatory revival. From 1992 through the present, District 14 has continually enjoyed a vibrant, enthusiastic, and well-funded local DFL Party whose members work energetically on campaigns for every level of office (and have fun in the process). Richard Ice, who managed several campaigns and later succeeded me as chair, played an especially key role in keeping the local party strong. We routinely delivered more volunteers for statewide campaigns and phone bank operations than did DFL Party units from neighboring districts. Democratic statewide and presidential candidates may not have led the vote totals in our district, but they performed much better here than they would have if there were no functioning local party at all—which was the case when I first took over as chair in 1990.

Even the decade-long Republican lock on the District 14 legislative delegation had some offsetting benefits, at least compared to the Bertram phase, which did our party more harm than good. However much I disagreed with their politics, Fischbach, Stang, and Dehler were all decent human beings who did not threaten and slander people who opposed them politically. Once the Bertrams were out of office and their machine gone, the local DFL Party was able to make a fresh start: to actually stand for something instead of running away from the national, statewide, and sometimes local Democratic ticket under pressure from the MCCL or some other absolutist group. It is hard to explain to Democrats from outside the district how liberating it felt to have the Bertram brothers out of there.

In 2004, under new district lines, our local party succeeded in electing a good DFL legislator, Larry Hosch, in House District 14B, which now includes St. Joseph, both colleges, and my own residence in Avon. Larry is a socially conservative and economically progressive Democrat. He is pro-life but does not take marching orders from the MCCL or cave to single-issue politics. We have run strong candidates for the new District 14A, and I am optimistic about our prospects there.

We live in an age when people have become increasingly disconnected from, and suspicious of, political parties. Some readers may find it odd that I would devote so much time and energy to creating and maintaining an organization that many consider useless at best. Some may find it even more incredible that the viability of my local party would be as important to me as my own electoral fortunes. For it was concern for the health of my local party, not just my prospects of winning, that made me a legislative candidate in the first place.

I do not celebrate political parties for their own sake, and I am fully aware of their perversities, narrowness, and flaws. Political parties are a means to an end. What locally organized parties do, at their best, is enable ordinary citizens to participate in politics and to engage face-to-face with friends, neighbors, and rivals in a way they cannot easily do as mere spectators of distant, top-heavy campaigns. By fielding candidates even in difficult districts, local parties also make it possible for ordinary voters—including voters who say they hate parties—to have genuine choices at election time. In both of these respects the doorstep democracy I practiced as a candidate in 1992 was an extension of what I attempted to accomplish as party chair.

Steve Dehler, my 1992 opponent, stayed in the legislature for ten years. His record was undistinguished. He authored some odd pieces of legislation, for example, to make it legal to roll dice in a bar to determine who would pay for a round of drinks. The 2002 redistricting placed him in the newly drawn 14B in competition with fellow Republican Doug Stang, who received the party endorsement. Dehler later ran unsuccessfully for a county office. His legislative career seems to be over. But he remains a living presence in my own life story because of the turn of events that pitted us in an engaging and sometimes thrilling contest so many years ago.

Door-Knocking Democracy

In political time the year 1992 may seem ages in the past. Some people to whom I have mentioned this narrative ask, "Hasn't politics completely changed since then?" In some important respects politics has indeed changed, most obviously through the advent of the Internet as a tool of political communication. In political campaigns modern information technologies allow for much more precise identification and classification of supporters than were possible two decades ago. Mass media culture, in a shift pioneered by Fox and imitated by other networks, has moved even further away from the ideal of journalistic impartiality in its treatment of political issues and campaigns.

But the type of old-fashioned door-to-door politics I practiced in 1992 has not changed in any significant way. Internet communications may supplement it but cannot substitute for it. Changes in mass media culture have little effect on campaigns in which mass media is largely absent. The ever-increasing journalistic obsession with horse-race campaign polls does not affect campaigns where polls are never taken or reported.

Campaign practice at all levels increasingly employs highly centralized, expensive, precisely targeted, consultant-driven strategies. But this is all the more reason to pay attention to what these new techniques tend to displace: the kind of broadly directed personal canvassing once employed by local political parties and still practiced by thousands of legislative and local candidates throughout the United States. At this under-the-radar level an entirely different, and much older, form of political communication continues to take place, receiving scant attention from political professionals or political scientists. (In my own political science training no one ever encouraged me to pay attention to doorstep politics; my acquaintance with it came by accident.)

My own legislative campaign in a particular district fifteen years ago is of no significance by itself, and for a long time I regarded it merely as personal and local history. But some recent conversations within the discipline of political science — concerned with political participation, civic engagement, and democratic deliberation — suggest that the kind of politics I practiced in 1992 is still worthy of attention, and convinced me that my own observations were worth recounting.

I am not a specialist in electoral behavior, and my campaign for office was not a controlled scientific experiment. By training I am a normative political theorist. Much of what normative theorists do is ask questions no one else is asking, and encourage empirical political scientists to look at things they are currently overlooking. The modest aim of this conclusion is to point to doorstep politics and say, "We should be looking at this." And indeed some empirical political scientists have already begun doing so.

Democracy at Risk

"American democracy is at risk. The risk comes not from some external threat but from disturbing internal trends: an erosion of the activities and capacities of citizenship." Thus begins *Democracy at Risk* (2005), the report of the American Political Science Association's first Standing Committee on Civic Education and Engagement.[1] The report identifies three specific dimensions along which civic engagement is endangered: quantity, quality, and equality.

With respect to the *quantity* of participation, turnout of eligible voters in the United States is low compared to other democracies and has been either flat or falling over the past four decades. Arguably more significant, and certainly more pronounced, has been the sustained decline in forms of participation besides the act of voting, such as participating in campaigns, attending political meetings, writing letters to the editor, or expressing an interest in current events.[2] Some other studies highlight another significant indicator of declining participation: fewer people willing to be candidates for office and consequently the growing proportion of uncontested elections at every level of government.[3] Recall that I myself became a candidate because I could not persuade anyone else to run.

The *quality* of political engagement matters as much as the quantity.

"In a large, diverse, extended republic," *Democracy at Risk* observes, "citizens need to learn to cooperate across lines of racial, religious, political, social, and economic differences." Political engagement is not confined to the act of voting but also "involves learning about public issues and understanding the political system. It means being heard as well as being able to explain and justify one's opinions to others in civil dialogue. It encompasses the capacity to affect the agenda and do more than just respond to given choices." Though the quality of participation is more difficult to measure than its quantity, *Democracy at Risk* argues that political activity in the United States is "increasingly uninformed, fragmented, and polarized."[4] In its concern for the quality of democratic deliberation, *Democracy at Risk* introduces a theme that has recently engaged a number of normative political theorists who have sought both to describe the character of healthy political deliberation by ordinary citizens and to prescribe ways to improve our current deliberative practices.[5]

Finally, the authors of *Democracy at Risk* worry about *inequality*: "the uneven distribution of civic participation." The decline in participation is not equally distributed but is more pronounced among the young, the poor, the less educated, members of racial and ethnic minorities, and moderate and less overtly partisan voters. If current trends continue, "the decisions of an increasingly unaccountable political elite will reflect the interests of a smaller and increasingly unrepresentative pool of highly mobilized citizens."[6]

A wide variety of remedies has been proposed for the malady of declining civic engagement. Many of *Democracy at Risk*'s recommendations focus on improved institutional design, including eliminating barriers to voting, reforming the electoral college, creating more competitive congressional districts, and enhancing opportunities for citizen participation in local political institutions. The recommendations most relevant to the doorstep politics I have featured in this narrative are these two: "encourage face-to-face contacts urging voter turnout" and "provide more opportunities for deliberative engagement."

I develop here what is only briefly suggested in *Democracy at Risk*. I propose that the kind of "doorstep democracy" featured in this narrative be carefully studied by political scientists, and that in-person, door-to-door campaigning—by candidates themselves where circumstances and scale permit it, by campaign volunteers otherwise—be encouraged by political parties, selected as strategy by candidates, and expected and rewarded by voters. Doorstep campaign contacts—reciprocal communications between voter and candidate in person, where voter and candidate codetermine the discussion agenda—enhance the quality of democratic deliberation and might contribute even more if the practice were to become more widespread, consistent, and deliberate. And a doorstep campaign that genuinely attempts to reach *every* eligible voter in the district (whether registered or not) will also help counteract the "quantity" and "equality" deficits diagnosed in *Democracy at Risk*. One of the advantages of this proposed remedy is that it requires no structural reforms but instead builds upon an already existing practice within our political system.

The niche is, of course, an old-fashioned one, obscured and partly replaced by newer, more expensive, more professional, and less participatory campaign techniques. Campaign practice has been moving away from the kind of door-to-door canvassing that was once widely practiced by political parties and that I myself intensively practiced in 1992. And yet the most recent, comprehensive, and carefully designed empirical studies demonstrate that the newer techniques favored by political professionals are less effective in engaging and motivating voters than the older technique of personal canvassing.

This argument is made most comprehensively in Donald P. Green and Alan S. Gerber, *Get Out the Vote! How to Increase Voter Turnout* (2004). The authors draw from a wide range (eighteen states and five election years) of controlled experiments of voter motivation techniques (including door-to-door canvassing, leaflets dropped at doors without contact, phone calls, mailings, mass e-mails, and mass robo calls to voters). The authors (both of the Yale Political Science Department) conclude that personal door-to-door canvassing is far more effective in persuading individuals to vote who would otherwise not vote than any other technique. "A personal approach to mobilizing voters is generally more effective than an impersonal approach. That is, the more personal the interaction between campaign and potential voter, the more it raises a person's chances of voting. Door-to-door canvassing by friends and neighbors is the gold-standard mobilization tactic."[7] Personalized, unscripted phone calling by trained volunteers was the second most effective technique. Direct mail had some effect in motivating an already identified partisan base but little effect on motivating infrequent voters or individuals selected at random. Mass e-mails and robo calls (techniques currently fashionable among some political consultants) had no measurable effect whatsoever. The other side of the coin, as the authors point out, is that more personal techniques like door-to-door visits are far more time costly for a campaign than impersonal, mass techniques, which carry a higher dollar cost but require fewer volunteer hours.

The studies on which *Get Out the Vote!* is based track the impact of various techniques on *whether* an individual voted, which is public record, not on *how* he or she voted, which is not public record. A candidate for office soliciting votes is interested in both whether and how an individual votes. But given the much greater effectiveness of personal canvassing in turning out voters, it would be reasonable for a candidate to assume that in-person contacts would work to his or her electoral advantage—especially against an opponent who does not do it or does it less.

The studies reported in *Get Out the Vote!* relied on campaign workers to make personal contacts. The authors hypothesize that a personal visit by a neighbor or by the candidate himself or herself will produce even larger positive effects on voter turnout. "Although we have yet to study the effects of candidates themselves going door-to-door, there is every reason to believe that candidates are as effective as volunteers, if not more so." They argue that studying the effects of such "super-treatments" as candidate and neighbor visits "represents an important new frontier in this line of research."[8]

There is a certain irony in the fact that a "new frontier" in electoral behavior research lies in studying the most old-fashioned of all electoral techniques and the one least in favor among professional political consultants. Green and Gerber point out, however, that the newer, more impersonal, expensive, and centralized techniques favored by many consultants have rarely been subjected to controlled experiment. The reason these newer techniques have been replacing old-fashioned door-to-door politicking, they observe, is not that the newer techniques are demonstrably better than the old (it turns out the opposite is true) but for other reasons. "The shift away from door-to-door canvassing occurred not because this type of mobilization was discovered to be ineffective, but rather because the economic and political incentives facing parties, candidates, and campaign professionals changed over time." Candidates and parties have come to prefer "campaign techniques that afford them centralized control over the deployment of campaign resources" and that make them "less beholden to local party activists." A new class of campaign professionals has emerged who have a financial interest in selling new kinds of services and in discouraging campaign methods like door knocking that generate no demand for their product.[9] To this we could add the effect of declining numbers of political volunteers, a point emphasized by Robert Putnam in *Bowling Alone*: as it becomes increasingly difficult to recruit political volunteers willing and able to engage in face-to-face politics, these newer, professionalized, centralized, impersonal, expensive, mass-communication techniques move in to fill the vacuum.[10] And, of course, this effect becomes self-reinforcing: the more political campaigns and political advocacy groups rely on impersonal and centralized techniques, the more the local volunteerism base will decline.

I agree with Green and Gerber that the effects of "super-treatments" like direct visits by a candidate deserve close study. Until such studies appear, I can only draw from my own fifteen-year-old intensive participant-observer experience with electoral "super-treatments." Voters do distinguish between personal visits by campaign workers and personal visits by the candidate. ("Well, you showed up yourself. That counts for something.") If the former is demonstrably effective in motivating voters, the latter will almost certainly be even more effective. Green and Gerber acknowledge that personal canvassing is extremely time costly for a campaign in terms of volunteer hours forgone from other activities. For candidates themselves, the time costs of going door-to-door are even more pronounced; this I know from experience. But this negative has an offsetting positive. When candidates themselves go door-to-door, *the time expenditure they are making is obvious to voters,* and many voters will take a more favorable view of a candidate obviously willing to invest time in this manner. (Recall voter comments on this theme in chapter 2.) An equal amount of candidate time invested in ways invisible to voters would not have this positive effect.

Someone concerned with declining levels of political participation and civic engagement might favor any political technique demonstrated to increase aggregate participation, regardless of which candidate or party benefits most. A candidate, on the other hand, is obviously interested in techniques that give him or her an advantage over an opponent. Increasing participation and winning elections are not the same thing, and there are indeed some effective election-winning techniques that depress aggregate participation. The argument has been made, for instance, that resorting to extremely negative attack ads may work in spite of — or even because of — their effect in discouraging many people from voting at all.[11] A precisely targeted phone or direct-mail campaign designed to turn out the partisan base may be successful even when it deliberately ignores the majority of eligible voters.

In the case of door-to-door canvassing, however, what is good election-winning practice is also effective in increasing aggregate participation and overall interest in the election. If increased participation is good for the political community as a whole, then in this case what is good for the community and what is good for a candidate converge. This is true for a number of reasons. If one candidate engages in an intensive door-knocking campaign, his or her opponent will be more likely to do the same. (I know of some incumbent legislators who door-knock energetically only when they have a challenger who is doing so.)

Another important feature of door-to-door campaigning is that one has a built-in incentive to contact a wider range of voters than one would do in a targeted mail or phone campaign. A campaign working from a good targeted phone list will not call anyone suspected of leaning toward the opponent. New residents not yet on the registered voters list or about whom no political profile has been assembled might not be contacted at all. It would be considered a waste of time and money to call the vast majority of voters.

When one is door-knocking, however, the incentives are different (and here it does not matter whether it is the candidate or a campaign worker).

It is possible, of course, to skip the doors of voters suspected of favoring the opponent, or of new residents about whom neither campaign has any information; that is, to bypass the same voters one would decline to call in a targeted phone campaign. But it will be obvious to everyone in the neighborhood that one is doing so, and this is not likely to help a campaign. And, as Green and Gerber point out, once a campaign has made the initial time investment to send a candidate or volunteers out to a neighborhood, it is relatively cost-free to contact precisely those infrequent voters whom campaigns otherwise tend to ignore.[12] Given that infrequent voters tend on average to be less wealthy, less educated, and in general less socially advantaged than frequent voters, a door-knocking campaign, by casting a much wider net than other campaign methods, may help counteract the *inequality* of participation that so alarms the authors of *Democracy at Risk*.

The authors also list a number of additional positive if less-easily-measured effects of a door-knocking campaign, all of which reinforce my own observations as a candidate: "Canvassing campaigns seem to encourage people to talk about the upcoming election with others in the household, which has the effect of extending the influence of a canvassing campaign beyond those who are contacted directly." Moreover, candidates and campaign workers receive "useful feedback from voters about issues and candidates," and the act itself of making a personal visit signals to voters the importance of political participation itself. "Many nonvoters need just a nudge to motivate them to vote. A personal invitation sometimes makes all the difference."[13]

So there is good empirical evidence that doorstep politics well-practiced might raise the *quantity* of political participation. But Green and Gerber's observations about conversations within households and feedback from voters at the door on candidates and issues introduce another equally important theme highlighted in *Democracy at Risk*: the *quality* of political participation.

Why Participation Matters

Why does the quantity and quality of political participation by ordinary citizens matter at all? Why seek deliberately to expand participation and enhance its quality? Why not surrender the field to the self-motivated and the already informed, and let the unmotivated or badly informed stay out of politics?

In answering this question it helps to specify the roles and duties that ordinary citizens are expected to fulfill in a representative democracy. The theory of representative democracy presupposes that citizens simultaneously *select, empower,* and *restrain* their rulers. This set of roles and duties is not simple but rather complicated, with several internal tensions that must be navigated. The full range of duties cannot be adequately fulfilled by a small minority of self-motivated and well-informed citizens. Nor can these duties be adequately fulfilled by a disengaged and badly informed majority.

Selection is the most straightforward and apparently least demanding function: citizens in their role as voters choose the individuals who will hold key public offices (and who in turn appoint other public officers). Technically this function is fulfilled as long as there is at least one candidate and at least one participating voter for every elected office. But elections are pointless unless voters have an actual choice among candidates, at least most of the time.[14] And we cannot assume that there will always be enough self-motivated participants (in this case self-motivated candidates) to guarantee contested elections. For there is a collective action problem here: an individual otherwise ambitious enough to consider challenging an incumbent might not run if he or she believes most eligible voters will take no interest in the contest; apathy usually favors the incumbent. And the more frequently elections are uncontested, the more voters will disengage. Genuinely contested elections depend not only on the ambition of a few individuals but equally on the engagement of the electorate as a whole.

It is not enough to vote individuals into office. It is also essential to trust them with enough power to accomplish what they were elected to do. No government—and certainly not a democratic government—can execute laws and policies without a significant degree of free, if conditional, cooperation by citizens in obeying laws and carrying out policies. And here again the function cannot be adequately performed by a minority of the most self-motivated participants. A minority may very well elect public officers in the first place (this regularly occurs in midterm elections). The public officers themselves, of course, constitute a small and highly active minority. But the laws and policies themselves will affect everyone, whether they have participated politically or not. At their best, election campaigns "pre-persuade" citizens to cooperate in the execution of laws and policies that were publicly discussed during the campaign. If a majority of citizens has had no participation in a campaign, their cooperation in the successful execution of laws and policies is doubtful. (For example, the man I met during my campaign who hated politicians, refused to vote, and favored national health care would probably be dead weight even to the policy he favored.)

Finally, the theory of representative democracy presupposes that citizens can also perform the opposite function: restrain excessive or abusive power on the part of rulers. This is, of course, a central principle of the Declaration of Independence and of the First Amendment guarantees of freedom of the press and the right of citizens to assemble peaceably. Adequately fulfilling this function presupposes a certain degree of civic courage in citizens that will not be readily found among those completely disengaged from politics. This function also presupposes that citizens possess enough knowledge about the political system and its underlying principles to be able to judge when government should be trusted and when it should be resisted—to fulfill two apparently opposed duties at the same time—and if resisted, how best to go about it. This function of restraining government and keeping it within constitutional bounds cannot be adequately performed by a small minority of self-motivated participants. Nor will an out-of-control government be checked by a politically disengaged majority.

And because there will always be a relatively privileged minority that possesses the resources and motivation to participate intensively in politics (and sometimes an interest in suppressing participation by others), low aggregate levels of political participation will reinforce already existing social and political inequalities. For all of these reasons, then, a representative democracy that enjoys only the participation of an already well-informed and self-motivated minority is a democracy at risk.

Democratic Deliberation

We have seen how door-to-door politics might increase the quantity of political participation. How might it enhance the quality of participation by ordinary citizens? There are at least two important, and practically interconnected, dimensions of quality here: information and deliberation.

With respect to the former: do voters have the basic knowledge about issues, candidates, and the workings of the political system to be effective and responsible participants? If so, how do they acquire it? If not, how can it be supplied?

Democratic deliberation presupposes political information but goes beyond it. It would be possible in theory for citizens to make political choices simply on the basis of momentary passions or unreflective self-interest. But democracy that was simply majority rule without reflection or discussion would not be a form of government worth choosing and defending. Public opinion polls could gather the same unreflective popular will more efficiently, and we could dispense with the time and trouble of holding elections. What distinguishes responding to an opinion poll from casting a vote is that the latter is an active choice in a way that the former is not. Choice presupposes deliberation. The choices we make, individually and collectively, at the end of a process of deliberation may very well differ from what we might have chosen without deliberation.[15] A system of representative government, like the one established by the U.S. Constitution, presupposes at the very least that members of the legislative body deliberate before acting. The choices voters make in an election are equally important and should likewise be the fruit of deliberation.

And true deliberation cannot occur in isolation: it requires conversations with fellow citizens. For even if one knew one's own interests perfectly from the outset—an implausible assumption in itself—in politics one's decisions affect others, and we cannot know others' interests without communicating with them. Political information and democratic deliberation are logically distinguishable qualities, but in practice they reinforce one another, and both are strengthened by political conversation with fellow citizens.

Information and deliberation, like participation, are rarely all-or-nothing;

even the most intellectually impoverished, mass-communicated sound bite or attack ad gives voters something to think about and talk about. The question is *how much* opportunity for acquiring political information and engaging in democratic deliberation our current political practices provide, and whether and how to provide more.

Samuel Popkin in *The Reasoning Voter* (1991) provides a relatively optimistic assessment of current practice. Popkin acknowledges that most citizens do not score well on standard tests of civics knowledge such as "which party now controls the House?" or "what the first ten amendments to the Constitution are called" or key facts related to foreign policy.[16] The reason most voters "are not particularly well informed about the details of public policy and government activities," Popkin argues, is not that they are unconcerned about decisions affecting the good of the community, or fail to realize that their individual interests are affected by collective decisions. The problem instead is that political information costs significant time to acquire, and when each individual's impact on the collective outcome is small, it is not rational to invest significant quantities of time gathering political information. Popkin claims that most voters rely instead on "information shortcuts" to decide how to vote without having to invest large quantities of scarce personal time in the process.

These information shortcuts include basing judgments on symbolic gestures, successful or botched, by candidates (such as Gerald Ford's ignorance about how to eat a tamale properly when courting the Hispanic vote), party labels, incumbency, and—most significant for our purposes—the advice of better-informed personal acquaintances. Some voters are better able to evaluate political information from campaign communications and news sources and pass their judgments along to others. "Uneven levels of political interest and knowledge, then, mean that an essential part of political dynamics takes place between voters. The campaign and the media only send the initial messages; until these messages have been checked with others and validated, their full effects are not felt."[17]

Popkin here reveals that direct conversation among voters is an essential element of his relatively optimistic assessment of voter reasoning. Mass media communications by themselves provide insufficient information for most voters in the absence of interpersonal deliberation. In seeking the advice of personal acquaintances Popkin's "reasoning voter" is active rather than passive. If this is true, then it is worth asking how the practice of interpersonal political conversation can be improved, even if one is relatively satisfied with current practices. But if it should turn out that the frequency of political conversation with personal acquaintances is *falling* in tandem with other indicators of civic engagement—and this specific question deserves study—then Popkin's own argument would have unsettling implications for the future.

Popkin's relative optimism about the availability of political information and democratic deliberation under current practice is by no means universally shared. Some analysts, as we shall see, perceive a deep disease requiring new and immediate remedies. But in any case it is worth examining how door-to-door campaigning by candidates—an already existing if out-of-fashion political practice—augments political information and encourages democratic deliberation.

Doorstep Democracy as Democratic Deliberation

By doorstep democracy I mean the practice by which an elected official or candidate for elective office initiates in-person conversations with as many of the district's eligible voters as possible, asks for each individual's vote, invites substantive discussion of public issues, and allows the voter to codetermine the discussion agenda. This was what I practiced in my 1992 legislative campaign. It is the practice encouraged by all the major political parties in Minnesota and engaged in—of course to varying degrees—by most serious legislative candidates in the state.

My definition of "substantive discussion" here is modest and easily attainable by any candidate and any voter; it does not have to be a Socratic dialogue. A one-sentence statement or question from a voter at the door about taxes, schools, health care, corrupt politicians, abortion, and so on, followed by a brief reply by the candidate and the opportunity for the voter to follow up if he or she chooses, fulfills this rather undemanding standard of political deliberation. What is challenging for a candidate is *getting to enough doors,* not the intellectual requirements of the conversation itself.

The standard here is broad but not infinitely flexible. It would exclude candidates who do not door-knock at all or make no serious attempt to reach a significant number of households. It would exclude candidates who initiate contacts only with an already identified base of supporters. It would exclude candidates who merely drop literature without personal contact, or who discourage discussion of issues even if the voter seeks to do so. It would exclude candidates who use the occasion only to deliver a canned speech without listening to a voter at all. These are not difficult tests to pass.

A voter who agrees to speak briefly with a candidate at the door enjoys an extremely time-efficient method of becoming politically informed: a good information shortcut, to use Popkin's term. Most methods by which voters gather reliable information about candidates and issues are more time-consuming than the act of voting and depend on the voter to take the initiative. Learning about candidates and issues from a candidate at the door (who initiates the contact) is, by contrast, actually less time-consuming for the voter than the act of voting itself. Doorstep conversation is of course very time-consuming for the candidate, but as noted earlier, this has offsetting advantages if voters notice and respect it.

The exchange of political information that occurs in a doorstep meeting with a candidate is, at least for the duration of the conversation, free of media distortions. A two-minute unfiltered conversation between voter and candidate may convey more genuine political information *of the kind that voter seeks* than an hour watching or listening to political ads or poring over stacks of unsolicited campaign mailings. In a doorstep conversation between voter and candidate, the voter has the power to codetermine the discussion agenda. Even if the candidate would prefer to keep it vague, the voter can demand substance. If substance is still not forthcoming, the voter has learned an important fact about that candidate and can take his or her vote elsewhere. A doorstep encounter is a two-sided interaction: life can be breathed into it from either end, at least if voters know they have that power and learn to make effective use of it.

Running into a legislator or candidate in the grocery store is not the same as having him or her show up at your doorstep, ask for your vote, and hear you out. The unspoken symbolic message, signaling accountability, as well as the actual conversation that occurs in a candidate-initiated door-step meeting distinguishes it from accidental or routine encounters among elected officials and voters. Nor is it an adequate substitute that an elected official make himself or herself "accessible" only for voter-requested meetings. (Any legislator who refuses even this is unfit for office.) Members of Congress, senators, governors—sometimes even presidents—are "accessible" to a voter who is willing to bear all of the substantial time costs, and sometimes financial costs, of initiating an in-person meeting. But in practice only the most politically committed minority will be ready and able to do this. In-person communications with a wide and representative range of voters will occur only if the representative or candidate initiates them.

It is important not to confuse the specific practice of door knocking with the more general existence of state legislative districts and local units of government. Levels of government "closer to the people" than Congress do not by themselves produce genuine conversation between elected officials (or candidates) and voters. The fact that an elected official or candidate *could* initiate in-person communications with the majority of constituents does not necessarily mean he or she will; this is still a major time investment. Some legislative candidates (including some secure incumbents) do not door-knock at all; some do it only when pressed by a door-knocking opponent; some make it the centerpiece of their campaign. The frequency of the practice also varies geographically within a single state and among states. In a state like California, where there are about five hundred thousand constituents per state assembly district, the distance between legislator and constituent is nearly as great as for members of Congress.

But the frequency of the door-knocking practice probably varies even across states with districts of comparable and manageable size.[18] And the same variability holds for local campaigns (city council, school board, and so on). Even for local elected offices in districts where it would be easy to reach most voters at their doors, some candidates door-knock, and some do not. And in some local campaigns, for one reason or another, door knocking is simply "not done." Thus, the frequently low level of interest and participation in local elections does not contradict my claim about the participation-enhancing effects of door knocking. It cannot enhance participation where it is not practiced.

In praising the kind of voter-candidate conversations possible in state legislative races, I am not necessarily arguing for increased devolution of responsibilities from the federal government to the states. That is a separate question and must be decided on its own merits. During the debate over ratification of the U.S. Constitution in 1787–88, the opponents of the Constitution—labeled the Antifederalists—argued that ultimate political authority—sovereignty—must reside in the states because they were closer to the ordinary voter than a distant federal government. And that line of argument did not disappear with the ratification of the Constitution.

I am not making an Antifederalist argument here. State and local governments are certainly essential to our system; without them we would be a democracy in name only. But many key decisions must be made at the federal level by elected officials who cannot be personally acquainted with the majority of their constituents, and I am not proposing to remedy this. If state and local governments were altogether annihilated or stripped of the power to decide anything of importance, it would be a different matter, but that has not happened and is not likely to happen. So long as *some* class of important matters are decided at state and local levels, doorstep democracy has a clear purpose and, if practiced, will develop and maintain citizenship skills in the average voter.

Nor am I arguing that representatives or candidates should simply "reflect" the wishes of the district. As a candidate one meets many voters who see representation in these simple terms, who believe the point of candidates going door-to-door is simply to collect the views of the district and then convey them to the state capital.[19] But doorstep conversations at their best are dialogues, not monologues from either side. Either candidate or voter may have something to teach; either may have something to learn.

Some readers of this narrative live in districts or states where door knocking is standard practice. For these readers I want to emphasize the significance of something they probably consider routine, and encourage them to make more effective use of the opportunity this campaign practice provides. Other readers live in districts or states where, even though numbers make it possible, one meets few candidates willing to engage voters this way. (In states like California where legislative districts are as large as congressional districts, doorstep campaigning could still be practiced by candidates for local office.) I encourage readers to look upon doorstep visits by candidates as *something to which voters are entitled*. If voters demand it, candidates will do it. If no available candidates are willing to engage in the practice, the solution is to search out and select candidates who will door-knock and reward them at the polls. Self-selection also works.

Doorstep Democracy Compared to Other Remedies

A question might arise at this point. Aren't direct interactions *among citizens* at least as important as exchanges between citizen and candidate? Shouldn't we be encouraging people to take the initiative to deliberate and act with fellow citizens, without depending on candidates at the door to start the process?

The answer to this question is yes: the most potent form of democratic deliberation occurs when people self-organize and form new types of horizontal, citizen-citizen ties. Examples here would include the 1960s civil rights movement—to which elected officials responded but which they did not initiate—and recent community organizations formed around issues of environmental justice.[20] Citizens mobilized around some issue or cause do not need a candidate at the door to start the process. On the contrary, the political power generated by a self-organized network of citizens will draw to itself office holders and candidates like bees to clover. (There is no denying that the Minnesota Citizens Concerned for Life was in this respect an effective grassroots organization in rural Stearns County.)

Thus, doorstep campaigning by candidates is not the only or always the most effective way to engage citizens. It is one way among others, with its own peculiar advantages and limitations. It does not come at the expense of other methods and may very well reinforce their effects. For example, a candidate's door-knocking visit to a particular neighborhood or small town may stimulate citizen-citizen conversations in its wake.[21]

All strategies for increasing civic engagement have their own advantages and limitations. Effective grassroots campaigns, for example, require qualities of leadership and quantities of participant-hours that are not always readily available. They usually cannot maintain their intensity over time without an infusion of new issues and new leaders. Their very success in getting a law or program passed may spell their decline as a movement when bureaucratic implementation replaces citizen activism. And a movement organized around a specific issue or cause might do little to engage citizens uninterested in that cause. In my district, for example, the hyper-participation of the pro-lifers had the effect of stifling, not stimulating, the political participation of everyone else.

One of the advantages of doorstep conversation as a mode of civic engagement is that it builds upon an enduring institutional structure—the practice of elections—and does not depend on any one issue or cause. Its civic-learning benefits are available to a wider range of the voting population than will be engaged by most grassroots movements. Most important of all, it continuously solves the motivation problem. As long as candidates for legislative and local office are persuaded that doorstep politicking is an effective vote-winning technique—and ignore those who advise differently—in every election year in every state there will be hundreds of individuals on the loose strongly motivated to engage fellow citizens in face-to-face political conversation. No other strategy for enhancing political participation solves the motivation problem so economically.

We should also keep in mind the sheer number of political conversations that can occur in a six-month campaign where a candidate visits somewhere between five and ten thousand households. Here doorstep democracy might be usefully compared with direct democracy of the town-meeting variety, another practice sometimes recommended by those seeking to enhance political participation and democratic deliberation by ordinary citizens.[22] (I do not refer here to direct democracy of the California initiative-and-referendum variety, which does nothing to remedy the pathologies of impersonal mass politics.)

The advantage of in-person direct democracy is that citizens speak directly to one another, rather than through the mediation of television, political parties, PACs, or the Internet, and directly vote on issues affecting the life of the community rather than attempting to persuade their representative to vote one way or another. If effectively practiced and reasonably well-attended, direct in-person democracy certainly would foster habits of citizenship.

The obvious disadvantage of in-person direct democracy is the limited scale on which it can be practiced, at least if one seeks genuine and active deliberation by ordinary voters. The state legislative district in which I campaigned had thirty-three thousand residents. This is far too large for in-person direct democracy. It works much better in a New England town of five hundred or so voting citizens, most of whom know one another and are willing to participate periodically in several hour-long meetings. Even in this case, the opportunities for *every* citizen to speak are limited. If we make the unrealistic assumption that all five hundred citizens participate equally in a two-hour meeting, each would have fourteen seconds to address fellow citizens. This is at the short end of the duration of a typical doorstep conversation between voter and candidate in a legislative district of thirty thousand. (And it is likely that at a town meeting of five hundred, a few citizens will speak much longer than fourteen seconds, and many not at all.) Of course, many political conversations can occur among citizens before and after the town meeting itself, but this is true of doorstep politics also.[23]

In short, whatever the merits of town-meeting-style direct democracy, measured by the number and length of opportunities it gives to ordinary citizens to engage in political conversation, the town meeting falls short of what can be accomplished by a state legislative candidate visiting fifty households a day over six months. And doorstep politics is applicable to a far wider geographical and demographic range than the New England–style town meeting.

Another proposal for enhancing participation and deliberation is the "citizen jury" or citizen task force. The idea here is to provide a small group of ordinary citizens access to information unfiltered by mass media and allow them to deliberate together in a face-to-face setting. In the Citizens Jury on Health Care Reform (1993) sponsored by the Jefferson Center, for instance, twenty-four randomly selected citizens spent four full days listening to speakers, watching videotapes, and conversing with one another. Other examples would include the Citizen Forum on Energy Structuring in the Pacific Northwest and a Texas forum on civil justice reform (1997).[24] The deliberations of such groups are typically reported publicly, and the conclusions citizens reach after deliberating together are sometimes contrasted with the results of an initial, undeliberative poll of the same group.[25]

I do not doubt that citizen juries enhance the deliberative skills of those directly participating. The question is whether they have any comparable effect on other citizens who are merely spectators. The citizens who most need to be reached are precisely the ones least likely to be following the deliberations of citizen juries in the press and who, if invited to participate directly in such a project, might be unwilling or unable to make the large time commitment. A citizen's thirty-second doorstep conversation with a candidate may appear trivial compared to four days of intense deliberation on health care, but the former reaches far more people and different types of people than the latter does.

One intriguing, if extravagant, attempt to overcome the numerical limitation of citizen juries is to convert temporarily the entire nation into a citizen jury. In *Deliberation Day* James Fishkin and Bruce Ackerman propose that two weeks before the date of national elections, all citizens be offered a modest stipend to spend an entire day discussing national issues and candidates in small groups with fellow citizens.[26] Local political parties would provide in-person representatives to make pitches and answer questions. Except for the timing, the stipend, and the attempt to bring opposing parties together in the same room, the deliberation day proposal resembles an idealized version of Minnesota's sparsely attended precinct caucuses. If deliberation day were to be instituted and drew widespread participation, it would be a gain for civic engagement. But given the low probability of deliberation day coming to pass, energy might be better spent reinvigorating existing deliberative practices, such as precinct caucuses and, of course, door knocking.

Internet Hopes

The Internet creates some truly new political possibilities and has already altered patterns of political communication. The near-monopoly once enjoyed by national newspapers and network news has been challenged by the rapid and unfiltered communication via the Internet of everything from suppressed truths to scurrilous rumors. The question then is not *whether* the Internet has changed politics but *how,* and whether it promises to remedy, reinforce, or leave untouched our sluggish practice of civic engagement.

So let us bring Internet politics—the newest technology—into conversation with doorstep politics: the oldest technique. The rationale behind the pairing is that both Internet communications and doorstep conversations arguably promise an alternative to the unidirectional, passive, hierarchical patterns of political communication fostered by mass media and current campaign practice. It is not my purpose here to discourage the use of Internet technology in efforts to revive civic engagement. On the contrary, I believe the Internet may be used in ways that complement and enhance the kind of face-to-face politics highlighted in this narrative. But we should beware of an excessive dependence on the Internet to the exclusion of other methods of engaging citizens.

Al Gore in his recent book *The Assault on Reason* (2007) exemplifies both the critique of mass-media politics and the enthusiasm for Internet-mediated remedies. In place of the founding-era ideal of a public forum in which all could participate and to which all could contribute, Gore observes, "today's massive flows of information are largely in only one direction. The world of television makes it virtually impossible for individuals to take part in what passes for a national conversation. Individuals receive, but they cannot send. They absorb, but they cannot share. They hear, but they do not speak. They see constant motion, but they do not move themselves."[27] In contrast to Popkin, who describes citizens capable of actively processing the information and images available through mass media, Gore describes a citizenry rendered passive: a "well-assumed audience" in place of a "well-informed citizenry." Gore's proposed remedy is an Internet-facilitated "well-connected citizenry." "The Internet is perhaps the greatest source of hope for reestablishing an open communications environment in which the conversation of democracy can flourish."[28] Gore is not alone in his enthusiasm for the Internet as a means of restoring an active citizenry.[29]

Others are more guarded in their assessment of the Internet's effects.

The authors of *Democracy at Risk* point out that the traditional wide-circulation daily newspaper serves as a "general interest intermediary," providing an increasingly heterogeneous democracy with "a shared focus of attention for millions of viewers and readers." In contrast, newer forms of media, including both cable television and the Internet, allow individuals "to create their own personalized versions of the news or avoid news altogether. . . . The 'interested citizen' becomes just another market segment to be pursued, a niche left to specialty cable outlets or political websites."[30] In *Bowling Alone* Robert Putnam (one of the authorial team of *Democracy at Risk*) observes that the Internet contains both the positive potential for computer-mediated "communication for civic engagement and social connectedness," and the negative "specter of a kind of cyber-apartheid" as the less privileged are shut out and the privileged communicate only with people who share their views and demographic profile.[31]

The Internet has unquestionably changed the ways in which political activists can be organized and how they communicate with one another. Howard Dean's campaign for the 2004 Democratic presidential nomination proved that the Internet could serve as an effective fund-raising medium. Equally important, Dean's interactive campaign blog enabled his supporters, most of whom had never met one another, to "bond" emotionally and reinforce one another's commitment in the face of hostile mainstream media treatment of their candidate.[32] The liberal activist organization MoveOn.org was created over the Internet and continues to function in ways very different from traditionally organized advocacy groups. Both the Dean campaign and MoveOn.org enabled Web-facilitated communication among supporters scattered over the entire United States who might never have met in person.

Two questions arise here. First, how effective can the Internet be in expanding political participation in the aggregate? There is no doubt that it can be used to organize in new ways people already motivated to participate in politics. Whether it can be used effectively to bring current non-participants into the process in significant numbers remains to be seen. Internet use has skyrocketed over the past two decades. During that same time period in the United States there has been no sustained upward trend in political participation and civic engagement. But it may simply take more than twenty years to discover how to use the medium effectively for this purpose.

The other question is whether Internet politics can be used to facilitate "bridging" political relations among citizens as well as "bonding" political relations.[33] To *bridge* means to communicate meaningfully with someone whose background and/or political views are very different from one's own; to *bond* means to communicate principally with those whose political views and/or demographic profile one already shares. Both bridging and bonding are essential elements of healthy democratic politics. The Dean interactive campaign blog and MoveOn.org demonstrate that the technology enables like-minded activists to bond in new ways. Whether the Internet will facilitate substantive communications *among citizens with widely differing political views* remains to be seen.

We cannot say that the Internet can never be used for bridging as well as bonding. The Internet is not an agent that "does" things or "chooses" a certain kind of politics. It is a medium that can be used in thousands of different ways for different purposes. Some of its possibilities have been fully exploited; some have not yet been discovered. And some recent developments in Myanmar (Burma) suggest that where public political communications are prohibited, the Internet can indeed bring together nearly an entire society in opposition to a repressive state.[34]

The practice of doorstep politics as I have described it in this work brings both voters and candidates regularly into conversation with fellow citizens who do not share their views. In that sense it challenges the bonding-only tendency of Internet politics as currently practiced in the United States. When I ran for office in 1992, most of my contacts were not regular Internet users. A candidate running for office today could probably assume that most doorstep contacts under the age of fifty are regular Internet users. But most eligible voters will not be using the Web to participate actively in politics. A candidate will never meet these voters in cyberspace. A door-knocking candidate meets many other eligible voters who do engage in Internet politics but who frequent Web sites with different political profiles than the candidate's. Over the Web the candidate might "meet" such a voter only by being the target of that voter's inflammatory attack; unrestrained "flaming" is less likely to occur in face-to-face meetings (though of course not impossible). In both of these cases, an in-person doorstep meeting is almost certain to be the first, and sometimes the only, meaningful communication between voter and candidate.

What the Internet now provides to a legislative candidate is the means of securing and deepening a contact first made in person at the door. (If only I had had this option at my disposal in 1992!) One or two in-person conversations over the course of a six-month campaign, despite their brevity, contribute something essential to our democracy. But even better would be one or two in-person conversations, followed by several Internet-facilitated interchanges in their wake. It is much easier to e-mail a candidate a question than to post a letter or initiate a phone call. Voters who say "yes, I'll support you" after the first doorstep conversation can be more readily connected to the campaign via Internet technology than was possible in 1992. Nothing will activate an individual with no interest whatsoever in politics; even doorstep conversations will fail in that case. But for a citizen with an initial, if vague, interest in politics who has been favorably impressed by a candidate at the door, the much lower time costs of continuing that conversation over the Internet might make the difference. Here is yet another "new frontier" in voter behavior worth careful study by political scientists.

The Spark

The political world has changed since 1992. I have changed. At times it seems I have been writing not about myself but about an obscure historical figure whose papers I discovered in some basement archive. Fifteen years ago my life's road came to a turn, and it was a handful of recounted ballots, not any decision of mine, that determined my direction. I marched on and have no regrets.

But in the course of telling this story it all came back: not just the sights and sounds, not just the strategies and conversations and laughter, but the whole crazy love of democratic politics that can sometimes overpower an otherwise normal human being. Our habitual political mood is cynicism. At times we can work ourselves up to a lukewarm sense of duty. We read about men and women who once burned with democratic intensity when kings sat on thrones and "consent of the governed" was a revolutionary idea. James Madison called it "the sacred fire of liberty." But all that seems a lost world. We look at our own politicians and at the campaigns of our own day and ask ourselves: sacred fire of what?

But the ember is still there, and small breezes can fan a flame. I caught fire once when I least expected it. And I saw a bit of that glow in the faces of people at the door. Perhaps they caught it from me, perhaps from some unacknowledged spark in themselves.

Acknowledgments

I had long intended to get this story on paper, but other projects always intervened. The catalyst for my finally beginning the work was a long conversation with Clare Ginger and RoseMary Safranek during a climb up Mt. Lassen in northern California during summer 2006. Somehow the fact of my running for office came out early in the hike. Clare and RoseMary pressed me for details and helped bring the experience to life for me again. I am grateful for their enthusiasm and for reading and listening to later installments of the project.

Erik Peterson and John Brandl read the entire manuscript carefully, and their detailed feedback immeasurably improved the final product. Erik and John, each from the perspective of his own professional expertise and political experience, helped me see that I had an important story to tell and challenged me to tell it more effectively.

My colleagues Scott Johnson, Kay Wolsborn, Annette Atkins, and Richard Ice read and commented on the manuscript at varying stages of coherence; their advice and encouragement kept the project moving forward at key times. Scott read multiple revisions of the introduction during the final precious days of his sabbatical.

I assigned a draft of this book to students in my Politics and Political Life class at the College of St. Benedict and St. John's University. The students' thoughtful responses and questions encouraged me to believe this story would engage new voters as well as old-timers. Some of the students have worked on campaigns and can tell door-knocking stories at least as good as my own.

My California friends Maria Henson and Ginger Rutland were gracious enough to listen to lengthy sections of narrative read to them at dinner gatherings. Maria helped me settle on the book's title.

Todd Orjala at the University of Minnesota Press was willing to look beyond what could have been an initial objection to even considering the manuscript: the passage of time since the narrative's central events. Todd read the story instead of carbon-dating it and judged that it had something interesting to say.

Steve Hoffman, Kay Wolsborn, and Angela High-Pippert, coeditors of the sixth edition of *Perspectives on Minnesota Government and Politics,* encouraged me to write for that volume a brief sketch on door knocking, "Politics the Ol' Fashioned Way: Doorknocking in the Age of the Blogosphere."

I am indebted to Brad Neuhauser at the Elections Division of the Minnesota Secretary of State's Office for producing on short notice a map of District 14A in 1992. I also received timely documentary assistance from Ruth Anderson at the Minnesota Historical Society and John Decker at the Stearns History Museum.

Pia Lopez has been my full partner in writing this book, as she was in the campaign, as she continues to be in my life.

I could not have written the story if I had not first lived it. And I could not have lived it without the help of dozens of campaign volunteers. Some are named in the narrative, while many others are not. I express my gratitude, undiminished by the passage of time, to all of them. There are no financial compensations for working on the kind of campaign described in this book: the only rewards are the friends you make and the stories you tell.

Notes

Introduction

1. For campaign manuals that emphasize door-to-door canvassing, see Bill Lofy, ed., *Politics the Wellstone Way: How to Elect Progressive Candidates and Win on Issues* (Minneapolis: University of Minnesota Press, 2005); and Jeff Blodgett and Bill Lofy, *Winning Your Election the Wellstone Way: A Comprehensive Guide for Candidates and Campaign Workers* (Minneapolis: University of Minnesota Press, 2008).

2. See, for example, the report of the American Political Science Association's committee on Civic Education and Engagement, which I discuss in my conclusion: Stephen Macedo et. al., *Democracy at Risk: How Political Choices Undermine Citizen Participation, and What We Can Do About It* (Washington, D.C.: Brookings Institution Press, 2005).

1. How I Got into This

1. At the time our party's local organizing unit was named "Stearns 16 DFL." It consisted of that portion of Stearns County that fell within state Senate District 16, which also included portions of Morrison and Benton counties and two sparsely populated townships of Pope County. Those parts of Stearns County not in District 16 convened elsewhere, as did those parts of District 16 that lay within different counties. A later senate district convention was held that included all counties and parts of counties included in the senate district. The system was just as confusing to participants as it must be to readers of this note.

2. For background on Stearns County, go to the Stearns History Museum Web site: www.stearns-museum.org. See the museum's historical pamphlet "Crossing Stearns County: A Sesquicentennial History, 1855–2005." See also the *St. Cloud Times* commemorative issue on Stearns County's 150-year anniversary, April 9, 2005.

3. Garrison Keillor, *In Search of Lake Wobegon,* photographs by Richard Olsenius (New York: Viking Studio, 2001), 12–19.

4. Kathleen Neils Conzen, *Germans in Minnesota* (St. Paul: Minnesota Historical Society Press, 2003), 44–45.

5. St. John's University, for men, and the College of St. Benedict, a women's college, are located five miles apart. They have merged their academic programs

but still retain separate residential campuses and institutional identities. Students ride shuttle buses back and forth between the campuses.

6. St. John's had over the years produced a number of statewide and national political leaders, including U.S. Senators Eugene McCarthy and Dave Durenberger. In the 1970s Ed Henry, a faculty member in the government department, served as mayor of St. Cloud. But in 1990 the political impact of the universities on the surrounding community was minimal.

7. For the rise and fall of the Bertram political machine, see "The Bertram Brothers," *St. Paul Pioneer Press,* March 17, 1996.

8. In 1990 large numbers of Republicans in my district refused to support Arne Carlson, the party's pro-choice gubernatorial candidate, who was running against a moderately pro-life Democratic incumbent. Carlson won the state but received only 40 percent in the district, as compared to 55 percent in the district for pro-life Republican U.S. Senate candidate Rudy Boschwitz; State of Minnesota, *The Minnesota Legislative Manual, 1991–92* (St. Paul: Secretary of State, State of Minnesota).

9. I no longer have Steve Frank's exact polling data from 1990–92. In a recent personal communication Steve confirmed this general characterization of his findings from that period.

10. In 1992 at least fourteen precincts in our county unit passed resolutions recommending that "Congress pass the Workplace Fairness Bill which will protect striking workers by not allowing employers to permanently replace them."

11. Gary F. Moncrief, Peverill Squire, and Malcolm E. Jewell, *Who Runs for the Legislature?* (Upper Saddle River, N.J.: Prentice Hall, 2001), 8–13.

12. "St. Joseph Candidates Face Off for Bernie Omann's Seat," *St. Joseph Newsleader,* July 17, 1992.

13. Audiotape of debate, October 6, 1992, St. Joseph, Minn., in author's possession.

3. Media Messages

1. In this respect my own campaign was typical of state legislative races across the United States. "About 90 percent of U.S. Senate candidates and about 70 percent of U.S. House campaigns use television. But television campaigns are not part of most state legislative races. . . . State legislative races tend to be fought doorstep-to-doorstep and mailbox-by-mailbox." Gary F. Moncrief, Peverill Squire, and Malcolm E. Jewell, *Who Runs for the Legislature?* (Upper Saddle River, N.J.: Prentice Hall, 2001), 76–77.

2. For a study focusing on *first-time* state legislative candidates — on individuals making that initial, difficult passage between private citizen and public persona — see Moncrief, Squire, and Jewell, *Who Runs for the Legislature?*

4. Dollars and Private Promises

1. The reader can verify this by doing a Google search of the phrase "obscene amount of money" in conjunction with the words "campaign" or "campaigns." Spending totals on state legislative campaigns vary widely across the United States, with some legislative candidates in California spending more than a million dollars and candidates in small-population states spending only a few thousand dollars. Gary F. Moncrief, Peverill Squire, and Malcolm E. Jewell, *Who Runs for the Legislature?* (Upper Saddle River, N.J.: Prentice Hall, 2001), 7. See also Gary F. Moncrief, "Candidate Spending in State Legislative Races," in *Campaign Finance in State Legislative Elections,* ed. Joel A. Thompson and Gary F. Moncrief (Washington, D.C.: CQ Press, 1998).

2. For examples of first-time candidates' distaste for fund-raising, see Moncrief, Squire, and Jewell, *Who Runs for the Legislature?* 83.

3. For full description of the program and an attempt to measure its effects, see Graham R. Ramsden and Patrick D. Donnay, "The Impact of Minnesota's Political Campaign Refund Program on Small-Donor Behavior in State House Races," *State and Local Government Review* 33, 1 (Winter 2001): 32–41. Donnay and Ramsden argue that the program had a modest effect in increasing the participation of small donors and might have greater effect if more voters knew about it. David Rosenberg, "Broadening the Base: The Case for a New Federal Tax Credit for Political Contributions" (American Enterprise Institute, 2002) reports a Minnesota Republican Party internal finding that the PCR program did not make individuals more likely to contribute but did increase the size of contributions. This is consistent with my own observations. Rosenberg goes on to argue for something akin to the Minnesota program for federal campaign finance.

4. *Manchester Journal Inquirer,* October 14, 2002 (the challenger was Republican David Odegard, and the incumbent, Democrat Mary Ann Handley); Web site of Republican challenger Bob Krumm, candidate for Tennessee State Senate District 21, www.bobkrumm.com/blog/2006/07/17/candidate-questionnaires.

5. For example, Woodrow Wilson, *The New Freedom: A Call for the Emancipation of the Generous Energies of a People* (New York: Doubleday, Page, and Co., 1913). See especially chapter 6, "Let There Be Light."

5. Abortive Dialogue

1. This episode is described in a number of sources, including Dennis J. McGrath and Dane Smith, *Professor Wellstone Goes to Washington* (Minneapolis: University of Minnesota Press, 1995); and Bill Lofy, *Paul Wellstone: The Life of a Passionate Progressive* (Ann Arbor: University of Michigan Press, 2005).

2. For an attempt to describe what democratic deliberation on abortion might look like, see Amy Gutmann and Dennis Thompson, *Why Deliberative Democracy?* (Princeton, N.J.: Princeton University Press, 2004), 73–76, 82–89.

6. Countdown, Recount, and Retrospect

1. On the local Bertram machine and its downfall, see "The Bertram Machine Takes a Political Hit," *St. Paul Pioneer Press,* January 15, 1996; and "The Bertram Brothers," *St. Paul Pioneer Press,* March 17, 1996.

2. "The Bertram Brothers," *St. Paul Pioneer Press,* March 17, 1996.

3. Newspaper interviews with this victim of Jeff Bertram's slander and other residents of the community suggest that Bertram's campaign to ruin an innocent person's life met with some success. "The Bertram Brothers," *St. Paul Pioneer Press,* March 17, 1996.

4. For the text and vote breakdown on the failed expulsion resolution and the successful censure resolution, see the State of Minnesota Journal of the House, Seventy-Ninth Session, Friday, March 22, 1996. See also my follow-up op-ed column in the *St. Paul Pioneer Press,* March 29, 1996: "Standard of Conduct Should Be Set for State's Lawmakers," where I summarized the argument for expulsion I made in my testimony.

Conclusion

1. Stephen Macedo et al., *Democracy at Risk: How Political Choices Undermine Citizen Participation, and What We Can Do About It* (Washington, D.C.: Brookings Institution Press, 2005).

2. Ibid., 22–30.

3. "Over the last two decades the number of office seekers in any year at all levels in the American body politic—from school board to town council—shrank by perhaps 15 percent." Robert Putnam, *Bowling Alone: The Collapse and Revival of American Community* (New York: Simon & Schuster, 2000), 42. See also Gary F. Moncrief, Peverill Squire, and Malcolm E. Jewell, *Who Runs for the Legislature?* (Upper Saddle River, N.J.: Prentice Hall, 2001), 9–13.

4. Macedo et. al., *Democracy at Risk,* 8–9; see also 32–27.

5. See, for example, Amy Gutmann and Dennis Thompson, *Why Deliberative Democracy?* (Princeton, N.J.: Princeton University Press, 2004); Stephen Macedo, ed., *Deliberative Politics: Essays on Democracy and Disagreement* (New York: Oxford University Press, 1999); James S. Fishkin, *The Voice of the People: Public Opinion and Democracy* (New Haven, Conn.: Yale University Press, 1995); James S. Fish-

kin and Bruce Ackerman, *Deliberation Day* (New Haven, Conn.: Yale University Press, 2004).

6. Macedo et. al., *Democracy at Risk*, 9–10; see also 36–40.

7. Donald P. Green and Alan S. Gerber, *Get Out the Vote! How to Increase Voter Turnout* (Washington, D.C.: Brookings Institution Press, 2004), 9. See also the same authors' description of their electoral turnout experiment in New Haven: "The Effects of Canvassing, Telephone Calls, and Direct Mail on Voter Turnout: A Field Experiment," *American Political Science Review* 94, 3 (Sept. 2000): 653–63.

8. Green and Gerber, *Get Out the Vote!* 40, 93–94.

9. Ibid., 23–24.

10. Putnam, *Bowling Alone*, 38–40.

11. On the strategic use of attack ads to depress turnout among less partisan voters, see Stephen Ansolabehere and Shanto Iyengar, *Going Negative: How Political Advertisements Shrink and Polarize the Electorate* (New York: Free Press, 1997). For a more recent treatment, see David Mark, *Going Dirty: The Art of Negative Campaigning* (Lanham, Md.: Rowman & Littlefield, 2006).

12. Green and Gerber, *Get Out the Vote!* 37.

13. Ibid., 38–41.

14. "The democratic system operates with an implicit expectation that elections will offer voters a choice between or among candidates, and by extension, between or among policy positions. Uncontested seats violate these expectations because they deprive voters of a choice. . . . Thus, the American system of government needs people to run for office in order to give voters choices." Moncrief, Squire, and Jewell, *Who Runs for the Legislature?* 2.

15. This is a point especially emphasized by James Fishkin in *The Voice of the People*.

16. Samuel L. Popkin, *The Reasoning Voter: Communication and Persuasion in Presidential Campaigns* (Chicago: University of Chicago Press, 1991), 34–35.

17. Ibid., 46.

18. This is a conjecture based on anecdotal comparisons between campaign practice in Minnesota and other states in which I have lived. Whether and how the frequency and intensity of door knocking as a campaign strategy vary from state to state and from district to district within states deserve careful study.

19. The difference between "delegate" and "trustee" theories of representation is discussed in Hannah Pitkin, *The Concept of Representation* (Berkeley: University of California Press, 1967). My own self-understanding as a candidate in 1992 was somewhere in between, probably closer to "trustee" than "delegate." But Edmund Burke, Pitkin's model of the "trustee" representative, did not engage in door-to-door campaigning.

20. See, for example, David Schlosberg, *Environmental Justice and the New Plural-ism* (New York: Oxford University Press, 2002), which describes the environmen-tal justice movement as a form of grassroots political participation that challenges the elite-dominated pattern of contemporary American politics.

21. Green and Gerber report evidence to the effect that canvassing campaigns, by encouraging people to talk with others living in the same household, can ex-tend their influence beyond those voters directly contacted. *Get Out The Vote!* 38. It is not unreasonable to assume that this same effect can occur in neighborhoods.

22. The nineteenth-century French observer of American life Alexis de Tocque-ville, in *Democracy in America,* was fascinated by the participatory and egalitarian character of the New England town meeting. An important recent work on the theme is Jane Mansbridge, *Beyond Adversary Democracy* (Chicago: University of Chicago Press, 1983).

23. Nadia Urbinati defends the citizen-deliberation possibilities inherent in representative government against critics who celebrate in-person direct democ-racy as the model of democratic deliberation. Urbinati observes that over the course of a political campaign, ordinary voters have more time to deliberate than they do in a town meeting and are not constrained by the "veil of unanimity and sameness" that often characterizes large public assemblies. Urbinati, "Represen-tation as Advocacy: A Study of Democratic Deliberation," *Political Theory* 28, 6 (Dec. 2000): 758–86.

24. For critical discussion of these initiatives, see Mark Button and Kevin Mattson, "Deliberative Democracy in Practice: Challenges and Prospects for Civic Deliberation," *Polity* 31, 4 (Summer 1999): 609–37.

25. James S. Fishkin, *Democracy and Deliberation: New Directions for Democratic Reform* (New Haven, Conn.: Yale University Press, 1991).

26. Ackerman and Fishkin, *Deliberation Day.*

27. Al Gore, *The Assault on Reason* (New York: Penguin, 2007), 16.

28. Ibid., 260.

29. One of many possible examples here would be Jerome Armstrong and Markos Moulitsas Zuniga, *Crashing the Gate: Netroots, Grassroots, and the Rise of People-Powered Politics* (White River Junction, Vt.: Chelsea Green Publishing, 2006).

30. Macedo et al., *Democracy at Risk,* 42–43.

31. Putnam, *Bowling Alone,* 169–80.

32. Matthew Robert Kerbel, "The Media: The Challenge and Promise of In-ternet Politics," in *The Elections of 2004,* ed. Michael Nelson (Washington, D.C.: CQ Press, 2005), 88–107.

33. On "bridging" versus "bonding" as contrasting forms of social capital, see

Putnam, *Bowling Alone,* 22–24, 362–63. See also Putnam's recent essay, "E Pluribus Unum: Diversity and Community in the Twenty-first Century," *Scandinavian Political Studies* 30, 2: 137–74.

34. Viola Krebs, "The Impact of the Internet on Myanmar," *First Monday* 6, 5 (May 2001).

James H. Read is professor of political science at the College of St. Benedict and St. John's University in St. Joseph, Minnesota. In 1992 he was a candidate for the Minnesota House of Representatives in District 14A. He has served as local party chair and has volunteered for many local and statewide campaigns. He is the author of *Power versus Liberty: Madison, Hamilton, Wilson, and Jefferson.*